GW00505627

PULP KITCHEN

Feargus O'Sullivan

PULP KITCHEN

Recipes for the Good,
the Bad and the Hungry

Boxtree

First published 2007 by Boxtree
an imprint of Pan Macmillan Ltd
Pan Macmillan, 20 New Wharf Road, London N1 9RR
Basingstoke and Oxford
Associated companies throughout the world
www.panmacmillan.com

ISBN 978-0-7522-2647-7

1 3 5 7 9 8 6 4 2

A CIP catalogue record for this book is available from
the British Library.

Typeset by SetSystems Ltd, Saffron Walden, Essex
Internal artwork by Sarah Coleman / www.inkymole.com
Printed and bound in Great Britain by
Mackays of Chatham plc, Chatham, Kent

Contents

Acknowledgements, ix

Introduction, xi

Gangster Movies
The Godfather, 3
Goodfellas, 7
Casino, 10
Scarface, 14

Fantasy
The Lord of the Rings:
   The Fellowship of the Ring, 21
The Lord of the Rings:
   The Two Towers, 24
The Lord of the Rings:
   The Return of the King, 27
The Chronicles of Narnia:
   The Lion, The Witch and
   the Wardrobe, 30
Harry Potter and the Goblet
   of Fire, 33

Romantic Comedy
When Harry Met Sally, 39
Annie Hall, 42
Bridget Jones's Diary, 45

Bond Films
Casino Royale, 51
From Russia With Love, 54
Dr No, 57
The Spy Who Loved Me, 61
GoldenEye, 64

Musicals
Oliver!, 69
The Sound of Music, 72
Singin' in the Rain, 75
Grease, 78

Horror Movies
The Silence of the Lambs, 83
Rosemary's Baby, 87
Scream, 90
The Exorcist, 93

CONTENTS

Comedy
Monty Python's Life of Brian, 99
This Is Spinal Tap, 103
Carry on Camping, 107

Science Fiction
Alien, 113
Star Wars, 117
Soylent Green, 121

Hollywood Classics
Casablanca, 127
Gone With the Wind, 130
Rebel Without a Cause, 133
Some Like It Hot, 137
Breakfast at Tiffany's, 140

The Razzies
Swept Away, 145
Showgirls, 148
Catwoman, 151

Foreign Language
Good Bye, Lenin!, 157
Amélie, 161
In the Mood for Love, 165
Together, 169
Women on the Verge of a
    Nervous Breakdown, 173

Historical Epics
Gladiator, 179
300, 183
Braveheart, 187

American Indie
Reservoir Dogs, 193
Short Cuts, 196
Blue Velvet, 200
To Die For, 203
Boogie Nights, 206

Animation
Snow White and the Seven
    Dwarfs, 211
Shrek, 214
Spirited Away, 217

Gay/Lesbian
Brokeback Mountain, 223
Bound, 227
The Adventures of Priscilla,
    Queen of the Desert, 230

Cult Films
The Rocky Horror Picture Show,
    235
The Wicker Man, 239
A Clockwork Orange, 243

CONTENTS

Asia Extreme

Audition, 249

Dark Water, 253

Battle Royale, 257

Bonus Features

Unusual Foods and Where to
    Find Them, 263

Recommended Chinese,
    Japanese and East Asian
    Food Stores, 271

The Pulp Kitchen Movie
    Collection, 272

Further Reading, 274

Acknowledgements

Of the many people who helped with this book, I owe especial thanks to:

My colleagues at *The Times*: Burhan Wazir, for useful guidance with the column that first gave me the idea for this book, and Alex O'Connell, without whose encouragement and enthusiasm this volume would never have been written. Bruno Vincent of Boxtree and Isabel Atherton of Watson, Little, for their invaluable help in turning a vague notion into an actual publication.

My sisters-in-law, Priscilla Hon and Rita Perez De Valencia, and my friend Joanna Hunter, for giving me ideas that turned into recipes. And above all, many thanks to my parents, for lending me their DVD player when mine broke, and turning a blind eye to my theft of their sugar thermometer, nutmeg grater and bain marie.

Some of the recipes in this book previously appeared in *The Times*, in the column 'DVD Dinners'.

Introduction

This book is the intertwined product of my two great obsessions: food and film. You see, my undying love of sitting in a darkened room watching projected shadows flicker across a screen is only matched by my fondness for swanning around the kitchen in a flour-encrusted pinny, rustling up meals to placate my bottomless gluttony. And over the years, as my interest in both cookery and cinema has developed into a profession, I've often found myself watching films as gripped by the characters' diet as by their impending doom or joy.

I wouldn't necessarily recommend this attitude to everyone. Once you start focusing on the food on view, I've noticed that your perception of the film starts to go slightly off kilter. Take *The Godfather*, for example. When after murdering an ex-colleague, Don Corleone's henchman Clemenza says to his fellow assassin 'Leave the gun. Take the *cannoli*', I found myself more interested in the cakes than in the Mafioso's callousness. Were they the type of *cannoli* stuffed with the standard sweetened ricotta, or did they have the less commonly found rich custard whipped up with Marsala wine? Either way, they certainly must have been far too good to leave in the company of a cheating stiff.

Likewise, when Hannibal Lecter mentions eating a census-taker's liver 'with fava beans and a nice Chianti' I didn't shudder, I just thought, What, a whole liver? – surely that would be too queasily rich for a single person? Maybe he invited Buffalo Bill in to try his victim on for size, and Bill had a nibble too while he was there, but someone who can thoughtlessly gorge themselves on such heavy food is surely safer behind bars, if only for their stomach's sake.

But while some sensitive souls might find these observations ever so slightly creepy, looking at cinematic grub can also give you a fascinating take on just how oddball the standard conventions of film actually are. While we rarely think twice about them, food scenes in films are weirdly detached from everyday eating. If we all ate as sparingly as people in the movies, we'd soon die of starvation.

Certainly, countless films include scenes of characters ordering food or squabbling over the dinner table, but how often do you see anyone actually put something in their mouth? Hardly ever. When film stars finally get round to tucking in, either they toy with their food – spearing a French fry for dramatic effect, maybe, or snapping a breadstick with pent-up frustration – or they gabble on with their mouths full. In the real world, this sort of bad manners would surely put a damper on the wild romantic lives film characters so often lead, as watching someone's dinner churn around in their mouth like a pair of Y-fronts in a washing machine isn't much of an aphrodisiac. At the same time, the convention makes sense. While an actress like *Showgirls'* Elizabeth Berkley is actually marginally more expressive when she munches than when she speaks, I generally find the sight of, say,

Humphrey Bogart talking considerably more interesting than the sight of him masticating. So I don't really mind if he leaves most of his steak on the plate.

Still, while food in films is so often a casually treated prop, in certain kinds of movie it takes centre stage. Watch a film with Italian, Indian or Chinese characters, and the kitchen is never far away. Movies like Ang Lee's Taiwan-set *Eat Drink Man Woman* let the characters' appetites provide a peek into their messy emotional lives, while in *Il Postino*, the poetic postman of the film's title flexes his literary muscles by rhapsodizing over the food dished up at his wife's trattoria. Horror films are also weighed down with celluloid calories. Given their obsession with the human body's vulnerability and its grotesque appetites, it's no surprise to find that monstrous edibles are such a feature of the average gorefest. Beyond the usual hordes of flesh-munching zombies, we shouldn't forget instances such as the shriek-inducing dish of Spam meatloaf Annie Wilkes (Kathy Bates) presses on captive writer Paul Sheldon (James Caan) in *Misery*, or even the chocolate sauce standing in for blood spiralling into the plughole in *Psycho*'s notorious shower scene.

In many films, food also plays a role in building up character, sketching in quirks which will surface later on in the storyline. Look on someone's plate in a movie and you often have the key to their heart. In *Taxi Driver*, for example, the first indication you get that Travis Bickle (Robert De Niro) is perhaps a few bricks short of a hod is when you see him ordering apple pie with a slice of melted cheese on it, a choice so bizarre it scarcely made me shudder less than the whorehouse massacre at the end of the film. And you learn all you need to know about Sally Albright's (Meg Ryan) mix of sensuality and control-freakery by watching the waiter's jaw drop as she takes aeons ordering dinner in *When Harry Met Sally*.

All of this rummaging through food in films gave me the idea for the book. With so many great eating scenes in cinema history, why not give viewers a chance to cook the same food as the characters? That way, while watching at home they could enjoy a celluloid meal at exactly the same time as the characters. I've expanded on that initial idea here to create recipes which fit snugly with the content, mood and period of many people's favourite films. And while food is the focus, in my commentaries on each title I've tried to shine an irreverent, sometimes slightly skewed light on popular films that we often love despite knowing that their scripts and storylines contain some appalling howlers.

I've kept my movie choices as broad as possible, with titles stretching from the neurotic tenderness of *Annie Hall* to the epic sweep of *The Lord of the Rings* trilogy, via the nudge-nudge silliness of *Carry on Camping*, so whether you prefer tender romantic comedies or hard-hitting Japanese thrillers, singing along to musicals or pretending you're James Bond, there's something in this book for you. And while a few choices in this motley collection of starters, mains, desserts and drinks are versions – albeit unusual ones – of familiar classics, the book also offers more arcane treats, such as ancient Spartan Black Soup, Japanese Bean Cakes, alcoholic Demon Bile, and instructions for baking your own sacrificial gingerbread wicker man. As a rule of thumb, I've avoided many of the most obvious foodie film choices: after all, you don't really need a book to tell you that a viewing of *Chocolat*, for example, might be complemented nicely by a boxful of pralines.

Everyone enjoys slumping in front of a DVD, grazing on whatever snacks are to hand. But now and then you want something a little more adventurous, and here I show you how to achieve it, turning an evening's viewing into a special occasion. I hope you enjoy working your way through this book as much as I enjoyed writing it.

Unless otherwise stated, all recipes are for four people. A list of suppliers for the harder-to-find ingredients (and much else besides) can be found in the Bonus Features section at the back of the book.

The Godfather

(Francis Ford Coppola, 1972)

A truly professional Mafioso never lets a little light murder spoil his appetite. One moment mob killer Pete Clemenza (Richard Castellano) is wiping bits of his erstwhile colleague's brain off a parcel of cakes ordered by his wife, the next he's cheerfully instructing war hero and reluctant Don-in-waiting Michael Corleone (Al Pacino) on the finer points of cooking for twenty mobsters. Michael, understandably, is not in the mood. His father, family boss and everybody's 'godfather' Don Vito Corleone (Marlon Brando) has just been gunned down buying oranges at a fruit stall. The Don is left gasping for life – though as he already speaks with a throaty rasp that makes him sound like he's swallowed a lump of chalk, it's a wonder anyone notices.

Despite his dad's fondness for leaving severed animal heads the way other people leave business cards, Michael clearly has a soft spot for the old bugger. Overcoming his long-standing repugnance for the bloodier side of the family business, he decides to seek out his father's murderers and square things with the other New York gang families. Evidently he likes his veal bloody, as he perforates his father's pursuers across the table at a truce meal, then flees to Italy to wait for the aftermath of the killings to blow over.

Michael takes a break from all the violence by blowing holes in rabbits in the Sicilian countryside, but back home things are still boiling over. The Don recovers from his wounds, but Michael's hot-headed brother Sonny (James Caan) is the next member of the family to be ventilated. And when the previously mute wife he has picked up in Sicily is blown up only a few minutes after speaking her first lines (Sicilians loathe a chatty woman), Michael finally accepts fate. Taking over as head of the family firm, he resigns himself to the endless Mafia cycle of heavy meals, gruesome murders and gaudy weddings. Now almost as stiff-shouldered and husky-voiced as his father, it's only a matter of time before he turns all the Corleone family's competition into pie meat and confetti.

This is as close to the recipe Clemenza recites to Michael as I could make it, though I must confess the onion in the sauce is an addition. Change it further if you like – but check your pets' heads are still attached to their bodies afterwards. Just a friendly warning.

Clemenza's Sicilian Meatballs

1 thick slice stale white bread,
   crusts removed

4 tablespoons milk

either 600g (21 oz) minced veal,
   or 300g (10½ oz) minced beef
   plus 300g (10½ oz) minced
   pork

100g (4 oz) pecorino cheese,
   grated

1 heaped tablespoon flat-leaf
   parsley, finely chopped

1 teaspoon oregano

1 small onion, grated

1 clove garlic, chopped

1 egg

¼ teaspoon nutmeg

salt and pepper

a little oil

For the sauce:

400g (14 oz) plum tomatoes

2 tablespoons olive oil

1 medium onion, chopped

2 cloves garlic, chopped

1 small glass red wine

1 small glass stock

½ teaspoon brown sugar

1 tablespoon tomato purée

1 tablespoon basil leaves

Start with the sauce. If you are using fresh tomatoes, score a little cross in the skin of each, then scald them briefly with boiling water and remove the skins. Heat the olive oil in a pan and soften the onion gently until it starts to turn translucent. Add the garlic and fry another minute. Chop the tomatoes finely and add to the pan. When they have softened slightly, add the wine, stock, sugar and tomato purée and leave to simmer very gently, stirring occasionally. The sauce can continue cooking while you prepare the meatballs, but add a little water if it shows signs of drying out too soon.

For the meatballs, soak the bread in the milk until it is completely soft, then squeeze dry and break into crumbs. Blend all the ingredients in a bowl, breaking up any clumps of meat with a fork, until everything is fully amalgamated. Dust your hands with flour, then roll the mixture into ping-pong ball-sized lumps in the palm of your hand. Fry these on both sides until brown and slightly crispy, then dry off on kitchen paper. Add the meatballs to the sauce and cook for a further 15 minutes.

By this time, the sauce should be reduced enough to coat the meat thickly (boil it down under a high heat if it's still too runny, stirring all the time). Remove from the heat, chop the basil and stir it in. Serve ladled over spaghetti.

Goodfellas

(Martin Scorsese, 1990)

The life of your average gangster doesn't seem that bad. Sure, there's the constant fear for your life, the hassle of regularly cleaning bits of slaughtered rivals out of your tyre treads and the burden of living surrounded by unbelievably garish home furnishings. But apart from all those pleasures, there are more: beating up anyone you want to, throwing cocaine around like icing sugar, wearing crocodile shoes and knowing no one will dare giggle at you – and food. Judging by *Goodfellas*, decent grub matters so much to wise guys that they won't even let their standards slip in the can. Rookie mobster Henry Hill (Ray Liotta) is sent down for the first time when he and his partner Jimmy Conway (Robert De Niro) get done for dangling a debtor in a lion's cage at the zoo. But while the average Joes inside have a rough time, Mafia prisoners have separate quarters, lobster on ice and all the drugs they can sell. It's not all luxury, though – without a proper garlic crusher, the poor felons have to slice their garlic with a razor blade.

But it's when Harry gets out that the real sweat begins. In prison he's developed a profitable sideline dealing coke with some partners in Pittsburgh. Back on the streets, his new-found little earner goes so well that he invites best friends Jimmy

Jimmy and psychotic show-off Tommy DeVito (Joe Pesci) to join him on the racket. But with mob boss Paulie (Paul Sorvino) breathing down his neck, gore-soaked neurotics for partners, his wife and mistress losing themselves in a blizzard of white-powder-fuelled paranoia and a blaring retro rock soundtrack blasting out from nowhere whenever he goes near his car, just how much longer can he hold his dangerous game together?

This recipe employs the famous garlic-razoring technique Boss Paulie developed in prison, to make an intense gremolata for sharpening up slow-baked veal shank. Slice it thinly enough and it will disappear into the sauce as completely as an informer into the witness-protection programme.

Osso Buco with Razored Garlic Gremolata

4 sticks celery

3 small onions

4 carrots

a little olive oil

50g (2 oz) butter

4 slices veal shank, bone in

flour for tossing

1 glass dry white wine

400ml (14 fl oz) good meat stock

2 bay leaves

1 bouquet garni *or* 1 tablespoon
   mixed rosemary and thyme

1 tin plum tomatoes, finely
   chopped

4 juniper berries (optional)

GANGSTER MOVIES

For the gremolata

zest of 1 lemon   2 tablespoons flat-leaf parsley
5 cloves garlic

Strip the celery of its strings, then peel and chop all the vegetables except the tomatoes into small dice. Heat the olive oil in a heavy-bottomed casserole with a tight-fitting lid, then melt the butter in it. Toss the veal in the flour, shake free of any excess, then place in the hot butter. Brown on both sides over a medium-high flame, then add the diced vegetables. Reduce the heat and cook for a few minutes, until the onion softens. Add the wine and scrape any meat juices off the pan bottom as it bubbles down. Add the stock, herbs, juniper berries and tomatoes and boil a few minutes more. Cover the casserole and place in an oven preheated to 200°C/400°F/Mark 6 for 90 minutes.

Meanwhile, make the gremolata. Blanch the lemon zest in boiling water and cut into very thin strips. Using a razor blade or very fine knife, slice the garlic so thinly it is almost transparent. Chop the parsley finely and mix with the garlic and zest. Remove the veal from the oven and stir in the gremolata. Cover and leave it to cook in the sauce for a couple of minutes before serving.

Traditionally, this is served with *Risotto alla Milanese*, but mashed or roast potatoes work well too.

Casino

(Martin Scorsese, 1995)

Despite sporting a wardrobe of fey pastel suits that make Barry Manilow look like Ernest Hemingway, mobster casino manager Sam 'Ace' Rothstein (Robert De Niro) is a tough customer who considers shattering a cheating gambler's hand with a hammer a gentle warning. A behind-the-scenes string-puller at Las Vegas's Tangiers Casino, he's so meticulous about his job that he even throws a wobbly when he finds the kitchen's muffins don't all contain equal amounts of blueberries. Ace loves Vegas and Vegas loves him back. Freed from the ball-busting attentions the police gave him back in Chicago, nothing can top his dream of making a respectable business out of fleecing the gullible. Or can it?

Unfortunately the sober-minded Ace didn't count on two wild cards when he placed his bet. First, there's Ginger McKenna (Sharon Stone), a money-grabbing angel in a white mini-dress whose lust for lucre is even bigger than her hair. Ace falls for Ginger hard at the craps table one night, when he marvels not just at her vast hairpiece (which deserves its own credit on the cast list) but also at her ability to throw dice in slow motion. They marry, but he soon finds that, with her lickspittle junkie pimp ex-boyfriend still in the background, he can't control Ginger like he can his caterer's muffins.

To make matters worse, childhood friend Nicky Santoro (Joe Pesci), a borderline-psychotic Mafia enforcer, rocks into town to ensure the mob get their cut fully and regularly. Pint-sized Nicky seems to have wandered accidentally off the set of *Goodfellas* and wound up in Vegas unawares. As he's the sort of guy who'd think nothing of pulling someone's kidney out with his fingers for giving him a dirty look, Nicky soon starts attracting all the wrong sort of attention. Ace's real nemesis, however, lies elsewhere. While guys like Nicky who squish heads in vices don't faze him, the real power in Vegas lies with the cowboy-booted hillbilly desert hicks that control the state government. And whereas he can placate the tough Mafia muscle, the Marlboro Man look-alikes who really pull the strings prove to be considerably less stupid than their languid drawl implies, and can only be bought off with free chips and booty on the house for so long.

There are a fair few American muffin recipes around. This one just happens to be especially good – even good enough for a cake fascist like Ace Rothstein.

Cinnamon Crusted Blueberry Muffins

180g (6½ oz) self-raising flour
150g (5½ oz) granulated sugar
½ teaspoon salt
1 egg
1 teaspoon vanilla essence

80ml (3½ fl oz) buttermilk *or* plain
   yoghurt
70g (2½ oz) butter
200g (8 oz) blueberries

For the crumble topping

25g (1 oz) butter
50g (2 oz) soft brown sugar
20g (¾ oz) flour (plain or self-
   raising)

1½ teaspoons ground cinnamon

Plus

8 high-sided muffin cases (see p. 270)

For the muffin mixture, sift all but one tablespoon of the flour, all
the sugar and the salt into a large mixing bowl. Stir in the egg and
vanilla essence, then gradually add the buttermilk. Melt the butter
and whip into the mixture. Toss the blueberries in the remaining
tablespoon of flour (this stops them weeping too much colour into
the mixture), then add to the mixing bowl.

For the topping, rub the butter into the sugar, flour and cinnamon to create a powdery blend. Spoon the muffin mixture into the

muffin cases until they are two-thirds full, and strew generously with the topping. Bake in an oven preheated to 200°C/400°F/Mark 6 for 18–20 minutes.

Depending on the size of your paper cases, this makes 6 to 8 muffins.

Scarface

(Brian De Palma, 1983)

'I want the world, and everything in it,' proclaims scar-faced Cuban gangster Tony Montana (Al Pacino) – and he means it. After just a few years in the US, he's already clawed himself to the pinnacle of Florida's drug trade. Now he's hanging out in an ultra-exclusive club that looks like a ferry disco, and has built his very own pimped-up Cuban version of Versailles. With more wide-screen TVs than Louis XIV ever dreamed of, it has the sort of gardens God himself would create if he only had the money.

Fresh off the boat, Montana had to wash dishes to survive, but now he's moved on to cutting massive deals in Bolivia with the drug overlord version of the Man from Del Monte. And where he once had just a flick-knife to defend himself with, he'd now think nothing of demolishing half his house with a rocket launcher just because he was bored with the wallpaper. Still, it's been a hard climb: he's survived Castro's jails, expulsion to America, attacks by chainsaw-wielding Colombians and being snubbed on the dance floor by an undernourished but soignée Michelle Pfeiffer.

Alas, the life of a brutal death merchant and drug peddlar turns out to be not quite the barrel of laughs Montana hoped it would. Floating around in his vast bath like a dog turd in a paddling pool, his paranoia and his obsession with money start sending him round the twist. He's horrified to find his once pure kid sister Gina (Mary Elizabeth Mastrantonio) has been soiled by his filthy lucre, going out after nine o'clock in the evening and even letting a man touch her arse. And while he's managed to marry his murdered former boss's moll Elvira Hancock (Pfeiffer), she's already displaying Hollywood's version of the terrible effects of long-term cocaine addiction: pink-rimmed eyes and a slight sniffle. Not only are the police closing in and the Bolivians out for his blood, but his face is so caked in drugs he's starting to look like a scary clown. Now that Montana is on the slide, a waiting game begins to see what will collapse first, the crumbling edifice of his drug empire, or the ravaged lining of his nostrils.

With its huge sugar content, this unbelievably opulent Cuban dessert is probably the only thing in the world that's got more white powder in it than Tony Montana's nose. But although it's rich enough to be as unhealthy as the real thing, it won't make whole countries' lives a misery, fund ruthless criminals or, horror of horrors, give you red weepers and a cold.

Cuban Gold Bar (Tocino de Cielo)

750g (1 lb 10 oz) granulated sugar	22 egg yolks
700ml (25 fl oz) water	2 whole eggs
	2 teaspoons vanilla essence

For the caramel

3 tablespoons granulated sugar	1 tablespoon water

Plus

a sugar thermometer

Start with the main mixture. Place the sugar and water in a saucepan and bring to the boil. Simmer the syrup until it reaches 110°C/228°F on a sugar thermometer – roughly 15–20 minutes – then leave to cool to at least lukewarmth, which may take up to 2 hours.

For the caramel, boil the sugar and water until they are golden-brown. Coat the bottom of a loaf tin with the caramel and leave to harden.

Beat the egg yolks and the two extra whole eggs until fluffy, then add the cooled syrup. Blend the syrup and yolks thoroughly using two wooden spoons, tearing apart any lumps in the syrup. Stir in the vanilla essence and pour everything into the caramel-lined loaf tin. Place the tin in a baking pan half-filled with hot water in the centre of an oven preheated to 175°C/350°F/Mark 4. Cover the whole pan with foil and leave to bake for 70 minutes. Remove from the oven and leave to cool slightly before turning out on to a plate.

Serves 8.

The Lord of the Rings: The Fellowship of the Ring

(Peter Jackson, 2001)

The Shire is quiet – too quiet. The homeland of the hobbits is such a cosy, bucolic place that you half expect a midget version of Mr Kipling to turn up bearing a plateful of cakes. Alas, peace is going out of fashion all over Middle-earth, and the hobbits' carefree days are numbered. When Bilbo Baggins (Ian Holm) leaves the Shire for a long ramble, he entrusts his nephew Frodo (Elijah Wood) with a magic ring. This is no ordinary ring, but a bauble of consummate evil, forged by the dark lord Sauron millennia ago to subjugate the whole of Middle-earth under the thrall of blackest magic. Now Sauron's huge eye gawps once more over the plains of far-off Mordor, and all the dark lord needs is his ring back to turn the whole world into toast.

To keep the ring out of the dark lord's clutches, Frodo is forced to leave the Shire with the Nazgûl, a gang of undead riders in black hoodies, hot on his tiny heels. Thankfully, he's not alone. Besides fawning hobbit flunkeys Sam, Pippin and Merry, he is shepherded by veteran wizard Gandalf (Ian McKellen). Unfortunately, the other big cheese in the world of Middle-earth magic, Saruman (Christopher Lee), has thrown his lot in with the big eye down south. A cosmic wig-out begins between the forces of good and evil, pitching

Saruman's sleek Brigitte Bardot-style 60s hairdo against Gandalf's shaggier, slightly more 70s crimped look.

While the hairstyles are battling it out, Frodo and co. manage to shake their pursuers and scrabble to safety in elvish Rivendell. There they form a fellowship with all the forces for good in Middle-earth, united to defeat Sauron's henchmen. They head south for Mount Doom, the only place where the ring's power can be extinguished.

But bickering breaks out amongst the fellowship soon after, and Gandalf disappears into a fiery crevice beating off what looks like an enormous steroidally enhanced cow, except that it has a chunkier tail and is permanently on fire. The hobbits press on, but with all sorts of rough beasts desperate to slide into pretty young Frodo's ring, the fate of all Middle-earth still hangs in the balance.

This spiced ale recipe harks back to the hobbits' happier days living it up in the Shire. It serves 4 people, or 8 hobbits.

FANTASY

Spiced Shire Ale

10 cardamom pods
1 cinnamon stick
12 whole cloves
1 or 2 tablespoons clear honey
water

1 teaspoon grated nutmeg
200ml (7 fl oz) apple brandy
100ml (4 fl oz) apple juice
2 litres (3½ pints) golden ale

Open the cardamom pods and strip out the seeds. Crush the cinnamon stick in your palm and place with all the other spices in a sealable container with the brandy and apple juice. Leave overnight to allow the brandy to absorb all of the spices' flavours. Depending on your personal taste, take 1 or 2 tablespoons of honey and dilute it with a little very hot water until it is easy to pour. Strain the brandy mixture into the liquid honey and mix well. Divide the spiced spirit between four tankards and fill to the brim with the beer.

The Lord of the Rings: The Two Towers

(Peter Jackson, 2002)

Exactly why has Frodo been chosen to guard the ring? The pint-sized hero may not be easily corruptible, but whenever he is attacked, all he seems to do is flap around like a big girl's blouse and wait for someone to save him. In the second instalment of the trilogy, Sam has to leap in as usual when Gollum, the ring's warped former custodian, jumps Frodo in an attempt to regain his long-lost prrrrrecious. They overpower him, but decide that the scrawny little schemer is more use as a guide than as dinner, and so free him to lead the way to Mordor.

Meanwhile, Sauron and Saruman are martialling armies full of uncouth cockney orcs and nasty dark-skinned turbaned people who probably have unsavoury toilet habits, planning to overrun the kingdom of Rohan. Ageing King Théoden (Bernard Hill) seems more concerned with his pipe and slippers than warding off the Evil One, but is roused to action when a spell on him is lifted by Gandalf. Yes, that's right – Gandalf's alive! Don't ask why, it's too complicated. Théoden's men fight for their lives in a massive showdown at the Hornburg fortress, facing off the dark side's unwashed masses with a troupe of appropriately posh and Aryan-looking elves. Their forces, alas, are no match for massive

CGI explosions and unending ranks of gurning cannon fodder. It is only Gandalf riding in at the last minute with reinforcements that manages to save the people of Rohan from being completely squelched.

Up in Isengard, Saruman is under attack from some talking bushes. Frodo's hobbit companions Pippin and Merry have persuaded the trees of Fangorn Forest to attack the wizard, who chopped up their relatives for firewood. Despite awesome powers, Saruman has neglected one chink in his armour – a high dam above his base so flimsy it can be toppled by a quick prod from a babbling twig. Saruman's tower and forges are swamped by water, and the powers of darkness are held at bay. But with Frodo looking increasingly twitchy and dirty-faced, how much longer can his pure heart hold out against the ring's evil magnetism?

The rings we normally associate with hobbits aren't on top of a cooker, but Sam does cook up a mean-looking rabbit stew on the trek to Mordor. This is a delicious, (Middle-) earthy version of his casserole, with crème fraiche added to counterbalance the meat's slight dryness.

Rabbit and Root Stew

meat of 1 rabbit, cut into chunks	olive oil
400ml (14 fl oz) cider	50g (2 oz) butter
4 carrots	2 bay leaves
12 small shallots	1 heaped teaspoon chopped
½ bulb celeriac	fresh thyme
4 turnips	200ml (7 fl oz) vegetable stock
1 cooking apple, peeled and	100ml (4 fl oz) crème fraiche
cored	1 tablespoon capers

Cover the rabbit chunks with the cider and leave overnight. Remove and dry off with kitchen paper. Peel the vegetables and cut them and the apple into small dice. Heat some olive oil in an earthenware casserole and melt the butter in it. Throw in the rabbit and shallots and turn gently until the meat is brown on all sides. Add the carrots, turnips and apple and cook a further 5 minutes. Add the celeriac and herbs and pour over the stock and cider. Bring to the boil, then cover the pan and leave to bubble away gently on a low heat for two hours, stirring occasionally. When the meat is tender and the liquid has reduced by about half, remove from the ring and stir in the crème fraiche and capers.

Serve with mashed potatoes to mop up the sauce.

The Lord of the Rings: The Return of the King

(Peter Jackson, 2003)

'THE RING IS MINE!' Has Frodo been turned to the dark side? As he stands at last over the flowing lava of Mount Doom, such is the ring's power over him that he can't throw it in. As he has already risked his life and his friendship with Sam and been spun into a shroud of silk by a giant spider to get this far, his affection for a trinket that looks like Ozzy Osbourne's engagement ring seems a little misplaced.

Back in Gondor, meanwhile, things are looking pretty bleak. Realizing their armies are too weak to defeat Mordor alone, would-be King of Men Aragorn (Viggo Mortensen) has decided to seek out and recruit the men in the mountains, a band of undead former traitors who live deep within a narrow crevice in the rock. Aragorn and company edge themselves slowly up the dead men's perilous crack, but the faraway city of Minas Tirith is already in grave danger from Sauron's black armies. Denethor, steward of Gondor (John Noble), has been driven mad by his son's death, and sends his remaining son out from the city on a foolishly perilous raid while forcing hobbit Pippin (Billy Boyd) to sing him some Enya.

Understandably this does little to soothe Sauron's massing armies, who bear down on the city walls with mutant four-tusked war elephants, club-wielding jolly green giants and empty-headed Nazgûl. Luckily, the assembled orcs are as stupid as they look. Éowyn, princess of Rohan (Miranda Otto), manages to kill the Witch-king of the Nazgûl, stabbing him in the no-face (why didn't anyone else think of that?), and the undead riders pour in to save the day in the nick of time, like a spookier version of the US cavalry.

Still, the good armies' travails are not yet done. They rush to the gates of Mordor to help Frodo by distracting Sauron's great eye – which, despite its size and consummate evil, seems to be pretty rubbish at spotting the hobbit twosome bearing in on it. The diversion works but, with impish Gollum stalking Frodo and Sam, determined to get 'the pretty' back for himself, the fate of Middle-earth still hangs in the balance.

This is my version of elvish Lembas bread, the food Gollum steals from the hobbits and throws over a precipice to implicate tubby Sam as a pie-guzzling glutton. If you are not a stickler for authenticity, you can use normal flour, but the buckwheat/semolina mix adds an intense, slightly gritty strangeness to it which makes it taste a little more, well, elvish.

FANTASY

Lembas Bread

250g (9 oz) butter
200g (7½ oz) granulated sugar
2 tablespoons honey
200g (7½ oz) buckwheat flour
   (see p. 264)

200g (7½ oz) semolina flour
1 teaspoon baking powder

Cut the butter into cubes and leave outside the fridge to soften. Cream the butter, sugar and honey together until the mixture is light and fluffy. Sieve in the flours and baking powder and rub them into the mixture until no large lumps remain.

Using your hands, bring the mixture together thoroughly into a single lump, adding a few drops of water if necessary. Split the lump into four balls, put these on to a piece of greaseproof paper and then flatten them slightly with a rolling pin. Using the heel of your hand, press each ball down to create a disc that is about the thickness of the top of your little finger. If any cracks appear, seal them back together with a finger dipped in water.

Using a knife, score but do not cut these rounds into 8 segments each. Place greaseproof paper with the rounds on a baking sheet, and put into an oven preheated to 150°C/300°F/Mark 2. Bake for 25 minutes. Remove from the oven and cut along the lines you have made while the Lembas bread is still warm. As it is rather crumbly when warm, wait until it has cooled fully before removing from the baking tray.

The Chronicles of Narnia:
The Lion, the Witch and the Wardrobe

(Andrew Adamson, 2005)

Never accept sweets from strangers – it might bring an imaginary realm in the back of an old cupboard to the brink of annihilation. This is the message of the first instalment in the Chronicles of Narnia series. The Pevensie children have been evacuated from war-torn London to the safety of a stately old country pile. But when a game of hide and seek leads them to a mysterious snowy world hidden in a wardrobe, they soon find themselves plunged back into another type of strife. Enjoying snowball fights, they little realize that Narnia – for such is the country's name – is currently the backdrop to an allegorical retelling of Christ's Passion story. Except with talking trees.

Family black sheep Edmund (Skandar Keynes) happens across the White Witch (Tilda Swinton), an imperious, dread-locked patrician in a dress that appears to be made of poly-urethane foam. The witch knows of a prophecy telling that four human intruders will loosen her evil grip on the place. She promises to give Edmund all the Turkish delight he can eat if he delivers his siblings to her castle. He tries, but they've all been spirited away by some talking beavers before the witch's evil, heavily American-accented wolves can sink their fangs in them. Edmund, however, is thrown into icy captivity.

FANTASY

The beavers lead the other Pevensies to Aslan, a lion as big as a garden shed, who heads the forces for good against the witch. His troops manage to rescue Edmund, who now fully realizes that trying to trade his kin in for treats was a bit off, even in times of rationing. But just in case the children in the audience don't yet feel guilty enough about liking sweeties, Aslan is forced to die at the witch's hand to atone for Edmund's mammoth sin. This does nothing to stave off an epic battle on the plains of Gondor – I mean Narnia – where a struggle unfolds between all the pretty, photogenic creatures on Aslan's side and the dumpy, misshapen ones supporting the witch. Thankfully, the mingers are dealt a death-blow and Aslan bounces back from the dead. All ends well – but will the Pevensies ever get back home?

This Turkish delight takes ages to make, but the result is quite delicious enough to be worth the temporary death of some trumped-up talking moggie.

Pistachio and Coconut Turkish Delight

750g (1 lb 10 oz) granulated
  sugar
1 litre (35 fl oz) water

2 teaspoons lemon juice
150g (5½ oz) cornflour
1 teaspoon cream of tartar

2 tablespoons rosewater

½ tablespoon red food colouring

100g (4 oz) toasted pistachios

100g (4 oz) icing sugar

50g (2 oz) desiccated coconut

Plus

a sugar thermometer

Put the granulated sugar, just over a quarter of the water (about 275–300ml, 9–10 fl oz) and the lemon juice in a saucepan and bring very gently to the boil without stirring. Using a sugar thermometer to test, heat the mixture to 114–118°C/237–245°F. If you have no thermometer, test by dropping a little of the mixture into a cup of cold water. It is ready when, on contact with the water, it forms a soft ball which keeps its shape when prodded. Remove from the heat.

In a separate pan, mix the cornflour and cream of tartar with a little of the remaining water to form a cold paste. Over a low heat, gradually add what water is left and bring to a soft boil, stirring constantly. Stir in the syrup and cook over the lowest heat possible while still keeping the mixture boiling for an hour. Stir regularly or it will stick. Finally, add the rosewater, food colouring and nuts, stir well, then pour out on to an oiled baking tray. Leave to set thoroughly overnight.

Cut into squares with an oiled knife and coat with the icing sugar and coconut.

Harry Potter and the Goblet of Fire

(Mike Newell, 2005)

Is Harry Potter (Daniel Radcliffe) getting his first stirrings in the trouser department? In *The Goblet of Fire* he seems as preoccupied with who to ask to the Yule Ball as with combating Lord Voldemort's Death Eaters. And while he's never normally one to recoil in fear, he suddenly seems nervous that girls at Hogwarts won't choose him for his personality, but only because he always knows just where to stick his wand.

Still, he's not alone: all over Hogwarts, students are going gooey over some glamorous new arrivals – students of the Beauxbatons and Durmstrang academies who have come to compete in the Triwizard Tournament. This inter-school championship pits three young sorcerers against each other in feats of daring and magic, and has brought Bulgarian Quidditch champion and general beefcake Viktor Krum (Stanislav Ianevski) and slinky French fox Fleur Delacour (Clémence Poésy) to Hogwarts to compete. So while Harry is grappling with his hormones, Ron Weasley (Rupert Grint) is pining after Fleur, and Hermione Granger (Emma Watson) is perfecting her high-leg kick (at the ball) with the dashing Krum.

As no Hogwarts contestant has been chosen for the

tournament, students over seventeen are asked to throw their names written on parchment into a goblet of fire, which will make the choice itself. At fourteen, Harry is too young to enter, so everyone (except the audience) is surprised when, after picking three, the goblet spits out a fourth name – Harry's. Though highly unorthodox, the goblet's decision is binding, and Harry is reluctantly forced to compete. Accordingly, he is pitted against foul-breathed dragons, stroppy mermaids and a hungry hedge in his efforts to win the cup. But that's not the worst of it – those dastardly Ku Klux Klan look-alikes, the Death Eaters, rear their shrouded heads again, forcing Harry to risk his newly pendulous appendages in a stand-off with fish-faced Lord Voldemort (Ralph Fiennes).

These sweet pasties feature in the film as a favourite off the snack trolley of the Hogwarts Express.

Pumpkin Pasties

500g (18 oz) ripe pumpkin, skin and seeds removed
50g (2 oz) sultanas
50g (2 oz) butter
½ teaspoon ground ginger

½ teaspoon cinnamon
2 tablespoons Golden Syrup
400g (14 oz) short-crust pastry
1 egg

FANTASY

Cut the pumpkin into small dice and put in a lidded casserole. Add the sultanas and the butter, cut into small lumps, and bake covered in an oven preheated to 175°C/350°F/Mark 4 for 45 minutes. Remove the pumpkin and sultanas from the pan and place in a fine sieve. Leave for a few minutes for the excess liquid to drain out, pressing the pumpkin gently with a fork to squeeze out the last juices. Remove the now drained pulp from the sieve, mash any large lumps of pumpkin that remain with a fork, and stir in the spices and Golden Syrup. Roll the pastry out thinly on a floured surface and cut circles out of it, using the imprint of a high-sided bowl to guide you. This should give you about 6 circles.

Put a heaped dessertspoon of the pumpkin mixture in the centre of each circle. Fold one side over the other and pinch the pastry tightly shut, creating a fluted edge to each pastie. Beat the egg briefly in a bowl. Brush the tops of the pasties with a light coating of egg and place them in the middle of the oven, preheated as before to 175°C/350°F/Mark 4. Bake for 15 minutes, or until the pasties are golden-brown all over.

Cool slightly, then serve warm.

When Harry Met Sally

(Rob Reiner, 1989)

Female orgasms are an exhausting business, if Sally Albright's (Meg Ryan) performance in a New York diner is anything to go by. When her so-far platonic friend Harry Burns (Billy Crystal) blithely refuses to believe any woman has faked orgasm with him, Sally decides to prove him wrong. Gripping the table as if possessed by an evil sprite, at first it seems like she's going to succumb to nausea brought on by Harry's hideous jumper. But then she simulates a yelping, chair-grinding orgasm so intense that its force could blow the doors off a transit van. With Harry unsure whether to offer her a cigarette or call an ambulance, it's no wonder a woman at the next table wants 'what she's having'.

Other men might be mortified, but the generally dirty Harry has got to know the normally prim Sally well enough over the preceding months to take it in his stride. Vague and mutually unimpressed acquaintances from college days, they had bumped into each other one day years later after splitting up with long-term partners. Sally was previously happy in her childless relationship with her boyfriend, as they could fly to Rome spontaneously or have sex on the kitchen floor without worrying. But when she reflected that the floor in question was clad with 'cold hard Mexican ceramic tile' and too rigid to make love on anyway, she got broody and dumped him. Harry's wife, for her part, waited an extra week before leaving him for a tax attorney, so as not to spoil his birthday. Still mourning their exes, the pair's relationship develops into something new for both of them, a non-physical friendship with the opposite sex.

Well, that's how it starts, anyway. Luckily for Harry, stumpy, mullet-haired death obsessives like him seem to be much in demand among the love-starved women of New York, and he starts going through Manhattan's singles at some speed. Sally dabbles in dating as well – but how long, we wonder, will it be until they catch up with the audience and accept they are obviously meant for each other?

In the volcanic diner scene, Harry and Sally are eating what looks like pastrami and smoked turkey sandwiches. If this were really what got her juices flowing, then Sally would be a woman easily pleased – salt beef doesn't quite hit *my* culinary G spot. Still, this Jewish/Polish salad, a typical accompaniment to pastrami, is definitely worth trying, pro-viding an interesting spicy relish to the cold meat.

Caraway and Horseradish Coleslaw
(Surówka z Chrzaniem)

½ head red cabbage

¼ head celeriac

1 large cooking apple

4 carrots

1 bunch spring onions

1 tablespoon grated horseradish

3 teaspoons caraway seeds

2 tablespoons dill

½ clove garlic, finely chopped

300g (10½ oz) sour cream
   (or mayonnaise)

juice of half a lemon

Quarter the cabbage, cut out the core and shred the leaves finely. Peel the celeriac and cut out the centre if it appears woody; peel and core the apple. Cut both into the thinnest julienne strips you can manage with a sharp knife. Grate the carrots and chop the spring onions into fine rings. Mix the horseradish, caraway seeds, dill and garlic into the sour cream. Combine all the vegetables and the apple in a bowl and coat thoroughly with the cream mixture. Cover with cling film and leave in the fridge overnight to let the flavours blend fully.

Before serving stir in the lemon juice. Serve with pastrami or smoked turkey, gherkins and mixed wheat and rye bread.

Annie Hall

(Woody Allen, 1977)

There's nothing like a bit of crustacean murder to get the romantic juices flowing. It's when we see Annie Hall (Diane Keaton) and Alvy Singer (Woody Allen) throwing lobsters at each other in a Long Island kitchen that we first realize how well matched they are. He's a whingeing, paranoid therapy junkie who makes Kafka look like a birthday clown; she's a gawky, borderline-frigid fruitcake who dresses like Charlie Chaplin and talks like a ten-year-old girl scout. Somehow, the combination works, and they share many happy times comparing sessions with their shrinks and enjoying four-hour documentaries about Nazism. Unfortunately, the glory days don't last. Alvy pushes Annie to better herself with adult education classes, but becomes jealous of the independent streak these help foster. She in turn finds herself clamming up sexually and starts to weary of a man who only gives her books with the word death in the title.

Things come to a head when they visit Los Angeles. Alvy loathes the sunshine, the empty-headed cheeriness and the diet of mashed yeast and alfalfa that all the white-clad pseudo-spiritual smiley faces they meet there seem to be into. Annie, on the other hand, has been starting to have a little success as a nightclub singer and gets the chance to cut a record, despite having a voice that quavers like a ninety-five-year-old woman who's hit the sherry. Alvy compares their relationship to a 'dead shark', and they agree it's best for her to head back for the West Coast. But with Annie gone, Alvy starts to realize that he's screwed up the best relationship of his life. The other women he dates (who are mystifyingly happy to go out with the physically unprepossessing and socially awkward Alvy) just don't have Annie's chaotic charm. Will he ever get her back?

This recipe refers, of course, to the scene where Alvy tries to frighten a lobster out from behind the cooker by confronting it with a nutcracker and a bowl of butter sauce. There are certainly more intricate recipes for lobster around than this one, but in my opinion it's still the best way to eat them – straight from the shell.

Steamed Lobsters with Beurre Blanc

4 live lobsters, weighing around
  750g (1 lb 10 oz) each
160g (6 oz) unsalted butter
4 shallots
150ml (5 fl oz) dry white wine
  (ideally Muscadet)

½ tablespoon water
4 tablespoons white wine vinegar
salt and pepper
1 teaspoon chopped chives
  (optional)

There are varying theories as to the most humane way to cook live lobsters. I personally put mine in the freezer for 45 minutes before boiling them, as this is supposed to send them into a painless sleep. When they are ready, place them in a steamer full of water on a vigorous boil, and cover. Cook them for 9 minutes per 500g/ 18 oz (the 750g lobsters recommended here should take about 13 minutes to cook). When they are done, set them aside away from the steamer while you make the sauce.

Cut the butter into small cubes. Chop the shallots very finely and place in a pan with the wine, half tablespoon of water and vinegar. Bring to a gentle simmer and cook until the liquid in the pan is reduced by half. Fill a small saucepan up to a third of its depth with boiling water and set to simmer on a low heat. Transfer the shallot mixture to a flameproof bowl and set it on top of the simmering saucepan, so that the steam beneath heats it gently. Add the butter cube by cube to the bowl, beating the sauce vigorously with a whisk as you do. Allow about 30 seconds' beating per cube, creating a thickened and aerated sauce. Remove from the double boiler and correct the seasoning.

Now pull the claws and tail off each lobster. Using a heavy knife split the lobster shells in half and remove any veins from the meat. Pull the shells off the tails and crack the claws with a nutcracker, leaving diners to pick out the meat themselves. Sprinkle the chives into the sauce.

Bring the lobsters to table, serving with boiled new potatoes to mop up any spare sauce.

Bridget Jones's Diary

(Sharon Maguire, 2001)

Aw, don't you just love Bridget Jones (Renee Zellweger)? She's just so adorably useless! A ditsy, drunken thirty-something publisher's PR, she has no idea how to do her job properly, speak in public, talk to men, cook, be on time for work, give up smoking or sing karaoke. In the real world, these flaws might be a little bit of a drawback, but thankfully Bridget lives in a wonderful fantasy England which bears only a faint resemblance to the one that actually exists. Not unlike the sugar-spun Paris of her continental cousin Amélie (see p. 161), Bridget's England is one where a lowly London wage slave like her can live in a sprawling Victorian flat above trendy Borough Market, where everyone's parents dwell in quaint little houses built in Cotswold stone and whose every last bit of grubbiness usually appears on screen blanketed in a prettifying layer of sparkling snow. Damn it all, even the men are better-looking.

It's men, unfortunately, who are Bridget's big problem. Despite entering her thirty-second single year, Bridget can't quite shake her knack of falling for 'alcoholics, work-aholics, commitment-phobics, peeping Toms, megalomaniacs, emotional fuckwits or perverts'. Her latest crush is on her sexy but reptilian boss Daniel Cleaver (Hugh Grant), who is probably all of those things rolled into one. Bridget believes she's turned him off completely by caterwauling Mariah Carey at the Christmas party, but when she comes in to work one day (late, bless her!) wearing a skirt so tiny Cleaver wonders if it's off sick, his interest picks up afresh. Before you know it, she's off on a mini-break with him, performing acts rude enough to get you tarred and feathered in some countries.

So far, so good – but almost as soon as they get together, the unctuous Cleaver proves himself to be a complete bounder, breaking off their trip to run back to London to a younger, skinnier woman from the New York office. All is not lost, however, as there's another possibility lurking in the background in the shape of dour, grumpy barrister Mark Darcy (Colin Firth). A childhood neighbour who last saw her cavorting naked in his paddling pool (as a child – not yet another drunken pratfall), he meets Bridget at a Christmas party back in her parents' cute snowy village. She makes such a babbling tit of herself that he damns her as a 'chain-smoking verbally incontinent spinster who dresses like her mother'. As if this wasn't cutting enough, she hears from Cleaver that Darcy once stole his fiancée. But as the shine on her slippery boss tarnishes and she moves jobs so as to shake him off, the stern-faced Darcy softens a little, and starts to look like he might just be made of the right stuff after all. But can Bridget keep her foot out of her mouth long enough to snare him?

As any fan of the film will recognize, this simple but delicious recipe is for the disastrous leek soup Bridget makes for her birthday dinner, which she accidentally dyes blue with some string.

ROMANTIC COMEDY

Blue Soup

2 leeks
2 carrots
3 medium potatoes
50g (2 oz) butter
2 cloves garlic, finely chopped
500ml (17 fl oz) stock

250ml (8 fl oz) milk *or* milk and cream
4 drops blue food colouring
1 tablespoon chopped chives
1 small (about 25g/1 oz) lump of blue cheese to garnish

Chop the dark-green part off the leeks and make a long cut down the centre of each one that stops just a centimetre (a bare ½ inch) before the head. Open out the leeks without breaking them in two and rinse thoroughly under the tap to remove any sand or grit. Shake dry and chop into fine rings. Peel the carrots and potatoes. If you have a food processor with a grater on it, grate them both. If you don't, just cut them into small dice. Melt the butter in a large pan and add the leeks. Cook them over a medium flame until they have wilted and are starting to seep a little moisture, then add the garlic and cook for a further minute. Add the carrots and potatoes, pour over the stock and bring to a boil. Simmer gently for 45 minutes, until the vegetables are very soft and the potato is starting to break up of its own accord.

Leave to cool slightly, then pulse the soup to a fine purée in a blender. Pour back into the pan, warming briefly if necessary, then thin the soup with the milk or cream. Add the blue food colouring and stir in. Ladle into four bowls and sprinkle the chives and a little of the blue cheese, crumbled into small pieces, over each one.

If you're preparing this ahead of time, cook up to just before you add the milk, and then finish it off when your guests arrive, as dairy products don't take well to being warmed twice.

Casino Royale

(Martin Campbell, 2006)

Lithe limbs, blond hair, an opulently swelling chest and a skimpy swimming outfit – could Daniel Craig be the first male Bond girl? Certainly, his tiny-shorted stroll in the seas off a Bahamian beach has become almost as celebrated as Ursula Andress's entrance in *Dr No*.

But despite being presented as eye candy, the reasons why Bond has hit the surf are anything but sweet. He's been dispatched in disgrace by MI5 to lie low after being caught on camera shooting an unarmed terrorist. Never one to stop a little business intruding on his pleasure, though, Bond also uses his Caribbean sojourn to stalk one of the operatives bankrolling the terrorist he shot. His trail leads him to arch criminal-cum-banker Le Chiffre (Mads Mikkelsen), an amphetamine-inhaling, blood-weeping sociopath so baroque he seems to have been borrowed from David Lynch for the film's duration. Le Chiffre's business is investing terrorists' money for them, and then sabotaging major companies to ensure that his shares perform just the way he wants them to. A massive jumbo at Miami airport is his next target, but when Bond foils the plot to blow it up and the company's shares stay buoyant, Le Chiffre is left with a massive debt to the sort of people who won't let him off with just a broken a finger or two. So how will he get the money back?

A brilliant gambler, Le Chiffre sets up a billionaires' poker game hoping to win it back, where each player puts down a $10 million stake. He chooses the suitably shifty venue of Montenegro for the game – but instead of being the dusty backwater with temperamental plumbing that it was when I recently holidayed there, the movie's Montenegro is a slick jetsetters' paradise full of decadently stylish hotels and deadly models that bears an uncanny resemblance to the prettiest parts of the Czech Republic.

Bond is sent to make sure that Le Chiffre doesn't win back any of the dosh he owes his terrorist clients. But he doesn't go alone. He brings along improbably slinky MI5 accountant Vesper Lynd (Eva Green), a whiplash-quick, sparkly eyed beauty who is as disdainful of Bond's methods as she is appreciative of his arse. At the card table both Bond and Le Chiffre play for high stakes, but as Vesper's charms start to penetrate Bond's tough shell, is his sense of pro-fessional detachment as much at risk as the mounds of taxpayers' money he so casually tosses on to the table?

This version of a classic Martini is invented by Bond at the card table as a way to distract attention briefly from the game. He becomes so attached to it, he decides to name it after Vesper, failing to take her hint that the name is appropriate because, like her, the drink's pleasures leave a bitter aftertaste.

Kina Lillet, as mentioned in the film, no longer exists as a brand. It is now called Lillet Blanc, and the quinine content of the drink which made Bond's recipe seem rather controversial (surely it would be too bitter?) was reduced in 1985. The current Lillet Blanc is a fine, slightly orange-flavoured vermouth. An online supplier is given on p. 267; alternatively, you can steep the zest of an orange in a bottle of normal white vermouth and use after it has infused for a week.

Vesper Lynd Martini

lemon zest
ice
3 measures gin

1 measure vodka
½ measure Lillet Blanc

Plus

a lemon zester

Using the zester, cut a thin, unbroken strip of peel off a lemon, and scrape off any pith on the inside using a sharp knife. Fill a cocktail shaker full of ice and add the gin and vodka. Shake well until condensation appears on the outside of the shaker. Pour the Lillet into a Martini glass, then tilt and turn the glass to coat the surface. If you like a mildly flavoured Martini, you can discard any Lillet that does not adhere to the glass. Drop in the twist of lemon zest and fill up with the alcohol.

From Russia With Love

(Terence Young, 1963)

Members of the evil crime syndicate S.P.E.C.T.R.E may be power-mad, ruthless psychopaths getting ever closer to bringing the world to its knees, but they don't know the first thing about matching food and wine. James Bond (Sean Connery) discovers this chink in their armour when tucking into a meal in the dining car of the Orient Express. He is fleeing Istanbul with the standard-issue icy Russian blonde Tatiana Romanova (Daniela Bianchi), who has defected from the KGB bringing an invaluable decoding machine along with her.

Romanova has been instructed by her superior to claim a deep love for Bond, but is herself a victim of another bluff, and hasn't got a clue who she's really working for. In fact, she has been duped into defecting by ex-KGB chief Rosa Klebb (Lotte Lenya), a recent S.P.E.C.T.R.E recruit and generally sour-faced baggage who brutally dispatches anyone who irks her with a poison-tipped flick-knife concealed in her shoe. Though he suspects something, Bond plays along with Romanova – that is, until his Turkish contact is killed. Then Bond forces some of the truth out of this hardened intelligence operative by giving her a gentle shake.

While on the train, Bond makes a rendezvous with a local

MI5 man, who is supposed to smuggle them and the decoding machine over the Yugoslav border. But when the MI5 man settles down to eat dinner with the runaway couple, Bond senses something is amiss. Surely no gentleman would be so ill-bred as to order red wine to eat with sole? Is this a genuine British agent brought up on the playing fields of Eton, or some nasty bit of rough paid by Bond's arch-enemy, criminal demiurge Blofeld, to steal the decoder and rub them both out?

As I'm sure many readers will agree, light red wines can actually go well with certain fish, provided they are not of the oily type such as mackerel or sardines. If, however, you wish to pass Bond's test of correct breeding, this conservative but highly effective recipe is entirely acceptable, and no doubt considerably more appealing than anything ever served up by Yugoslav State Railways.

Sole in White Wine

2 Dover sole fillets	1 glass dry white wine
plain flour	(such as Muscadet)
100g (4 oz) butter	4 tomatoes
4 shallots, finely minced	1 tablespoon fresh dill

Coat the fillets lightly in the flour. Heat the butter in a large frying pan and add the fish. Brown each fillet briefly on both sides, then add the shallots and wine. Simmer gently for 10 minutes. Meanwhile, score a little cross in the skin of each tomato, then scald them in boiling water for 30 seconds. Drain, peel off the loosened skins, and chop the tomatoes finely. Remove the fish to a covered dish. Add the tomatoes to the pan and boil until they have melted into the sauce. Pour over the soles and sprinkle the dill on top.

Serve with new potatoes and a glass of the same wine they were cooked in.

Dr No

(Terence Young, 1962)

Have you ever seen a praying mantis eat her own husband after they've made love? Chesty shell-gatherer Honey Ryder (Ursula Andress) claims she has, but then, with a name like a 70s porn star, her voyeuristic interest in watching insects getting it on is perhaps not so surprising. She is discovered by James Bond (Sean Connery, in his first outing in the role) trespassing on the shores of a private island off the coast of Jamaica, where he has come to investigate the mysterious death of a British agent.

When he hasn't been sampling the effortlessly acquired pleasures of Jamaica's women, Bond has been sniffing out clues into the unexplained assassination. He discovers a trail of evidence pointing him towards Crab Quay, an island owned by half-German, half-Chinese scientist Dr No (Joseph Wiseman). Alas, reaching the island is difficult, as it is shunned by the naive locals who believe a dragon patrols its shores. When Bond sneaks in and meets Honey on the beach, she supports the story, claiming she has seen the dragon herself. It transpires, however, that her mythical beast-spotting skills are less developed than her knowledge of the sexual kinks of carnivorous mantids.

When it arrives, the 'dragon' proves to be an armoured

car with a flame-thrower and some cartoonish fangs stuck on the front, which would scarcely pass muster as a float at a village fête. Despite its amateurish camouflage, the car's occupants manage to torch Bond's assistant, and ultimately capture him and Honey. They take them to Dr No's unfeasibly groovy, swingingly furnished lair, hidden deep within the island's core, where they are kept in what would become typical Bond-style luxurious captivity in a room tastefully lined with mink.

The icy Dr No entertains them over dinner with his subterranean aquarium and bone-crushing metal hands, but Bond realizes that time may be running out. Dr No is bitter that, despite his obvious genius, American scientists have never trusted or respected him. It's easy to see why: though he's supposed to be half-Chinese, he is quite obviously an Englishman who thinks wearing a bit of eyeliner and affecting a squint are enough to make him look Asian; having hands that look like a pair of PVC washing-up gloves doesn't help much, either. Anyway, having developed a lethal weapon to crush the Americans' impudence, Dr No is planning to wipe the smirk off their faces by crippling the space station at Cape Canaveral with his own homemade nuclear reactor. But can Bond escape his metallic clutches soon enough to destroy Dr No's infernal machinery and save the world for queen and country? Given that this is the first in the series, I'll leave you to guess.

Just like Dr No himself, this Cuban-Chinese recipe is an unusual blend of Caribbean and East Asian influences. While the sharp citrus juices cut through the meat's richness, the papain contained within the papaya tenderizes the steak so effectively that the meat might as well have been crushed into oblivion in Dr No's steely grip.

Asio-Caribbean Papaya Steak

1 papaya

juice of 2 limes

juice of 1 orange

2 teaspoons Asian five spice
   blend (see p. 264)

1 teaspoon chopped fresh ginger

1 green chilli, chopped

2 tablespoons soy sauce

2 large frying steaks

1 large bunch spring onions,
   chopped into rings

2 tablespoons chopped
   coriander leaf

Peel the papaya, remove the seeds and chop the flesh into tiny chunks. Put in a flat-bottomed dish and add the fruit juice, five spice, ginger, chilli and soy sauce. Flatten the steaks with a meat mallet and place them in the dish, coating and covering them with the papaya marinade. Leave in the fridge overnight while the papaya tenderizes the meat.

Remove the meat from the marinade and scrape off any fruit or juice. Put in a hot frying pan with the spring onions and fry until well browned on both sides (about 2 minutes per side). Add the marinade to the pan and simmer for another 4 minutes or so, depending on how you like your steak. Remove the meat to a warm, covered dish and add a quarter teacupful of water to the pan. Boil the contents until the papaya is very soft and the sauce is thick.

Pour over the steaks, sprinkle with the chopped coriander and serve with steamed rice and spring greens.

60

The Spy Who Loved Me

(Lewis Gilbert, 1977)

KGB agent Major Anya Amasova (Barbara Bach) is in a tizzy. She's been sparring with MI6 operative James Bond (Roger Moore) for possession of a secret microfilm, chasing around a whole brochure's worth of well-known Egyptian tourist attractions in order to get hold of it. She and Bond are sent to Cairo to track down the tiny slide when it is linked to the disappearance of a British and a Soviet submarine.

Though they are opponents, the pair have found themselves joining forces to fight off massive, metal-toothed assassin Jaws (Richard Kiel), who not even Bond's ever-so-slightly camp repartee and arched eyebrows can vanquish. Finally, Amasova manages to secure the microfilm for the Soviets, by drugging Bond when his guard is down. Using her impressive cleavage and distinctively wooden acting style to killing effect, she blows sedative smoke in his face. But having escaped with the miniature blueprint, she is furious to discover later that Bond has already scanned it and found it to be essentially useless.

It's not entirely without leads, however, as it contains one tiny clue: a stamp bearing the logo of international shipping plutocrat, Karl Stromberg (Curt Jurgens). Deciding that temporary collaboration is the best policy, their superiors send both agents together to check out Stromberg's aquatic base, floating indiscreetly off the coast of Sardinia. Dropping in on Stromberg disguised as a marine biologist and his wife, the two discover yet more suspicious clues, such as the delicately turned human hand floating in Stromberg's aquarium. But while the culprit in the matter of the submarines' disappearance now seems clear, many questions remain unanswered. What does Stromberg want with the stolen craft? Where is he hiding them? And if he wants to keep his dastardly plans quiet, why does he choose to live in a gigantic metal spider bobbing around just off a tourist-packed beach?

Fittingly, this refreshing and summery Sardinian dish of mullet left to stew in its own juices is as fishy as the contents of Stromberg's shark tank (but minus the human flesh).

Sardinian Mullet Escabeche

1 large grey mullet	3 cloves garlic, halved
plain flour	300ml (10 fl oz) passata
sunflower oil for frying	(sieved tomatoes)
150ml (5 fl oz) olive oil	1 bay leaf
150ml (5 fl oz) balsamic vinegar	1 tablespoon flat-leaf parsley,
salt and black pepper	very finely chopped

Have your fishmonger clean and gut your mullet. Dry it with kitchen paper, then roll it in the flour until nicely coated. Fry it on both sides in the sunflower oil, for about 5 to 6 minutes per side, then leave to drain on kitchen paper. Heat the olive oil in another pan, and fry the garlic until golden-brown. Remove the garlic and add the tomatoes, bay leaf and vinegar. Simmer for 10 minutes, stirring regularly so that the sauce amalgamates properly. Season to taste (the sauce should be sharp and refreshing). Put the fish in an earthenware pot and pour the still hot sauce over it. Once it has cooled, place the fish in the fridge overnight to marinate.

Sprinkle with the parsley the following day and serve cold. As grey mullet is a very large fish, this dish serves up to four people, or five as a starter. If you are serving this as a main, start the meal off as an Italian would, with a substantial pasta course beforehand. Then serve the fish on its own with some grilled vegetables and maybe a hunk of coarse-grained bread for mopping up the sauce.

GoldenEye

(Martin Campbell, 1995)

Is GoldenEye the most preposterous secret weapon in a Bond film yet? A vast Soviet satellite system that disables all electronic equipment within its target area with a nuclear ray, its entire mechanism is controlled by a little amber slide that looks like a boiled sweet. This deadly weapon has been squirrelled away in a Russian Arctic facility, secret and unused until, one snowy night, its guardians are paid a visit by dark forces keen to harness its power for nefarious ends.

These forces come in the shape of renegade Red Army General Ourumov (Gottfried John), a stumpy sadist who looks like he's had a malevolent sneer on his face ever since the midwife first slapped his arse. He's accompanied by sidekick Xenia Onatopp (Famke Janssen), a psychopathic vamp whose effectiveness as a stealthy agent of terror must surely be undermined by her fondness for demented cackling and for using her nutcracker thighs to crush lovers to death. Working for the shadowy Janus organization, the blood-thirsty pair mow down the station's staff and steal Golden-Eye, but not before programming it to destroy the facility. Unfortunately, they leave two witnesses to their identities alive in the burning wreckage – beautiful computer program-mer Natalya Simonova (Izabella Scorupco) and eminently slappable geek genius and comic relief Boris Grishenko (Alan Cumming).

Despite the remaining survivors, there's little to stop the arch-criminals from creating worldwide mayhem now they have the deadly bauble in their grasp. Little, that is, except an ageing British Lothario with a weakness for boys' toys, easy women and the flashier brands of champagne. For, yes, MI6 have put James Bond (Pierce Brosnan) on their trail. They've sent Britain's finest to Russia to track down the survivors from the satellite station, before the Janus organization can take them out of commission for good. And he comes in the nick of time. When computer whiz Boris turns out to be in the organization's pay, Simonova is lured into a trap only to be saved by Bond – who has himself just narrowly escaped being dispatched by old pincer-thighs Onatopp. But after a masonry-shattering tank chase through St Petersburg (where in a display of his characteristic flair and finesse, he decides that many of the city's historic monuments would look better knocked through), Bond gets an unpleasant shock. For it turns out that the evil mastermind behind the Janus organization is not the standard cat-caressing German or icy-hearted loon with a giant goldfish bowl full of sharks, but an old and once-valued friend.

While Bond's classic shaken Martini may be the perfect complement to a game of roulette, it's not really very practical as refreshment out in the Russian wilds. For this reason, I've created this alcoholic dessert as a version of his favourite cocktail, better tailored to suit the icy conditions of the sub-Arctic tundra.

Arctic Martini Granita

16 limes

50ml (2 fl oz) red vermouth

140g (5 oz) caster sugar

100ml (4 fl oz) water

400ml (14 fl oz) vodka

Squeeze the juice out of the limes. Remove the zest from 4 of them, cut into thin, pith-free strips and mix with the juice. Add the vermouth and leave for half an hour. Put the sugar and water in a pan and bring gently to the boil, dissolving all the sugar. Keep on a low boil for a few minutes, then set aside to cool. Put the vermouth, the syrup and the vodka in a container and stir well. Place in the freezer until crystals start to form. Break up any large blocks with a fork, stir and return to the freezer. Repeat the process at least twice until the liquid is all frozen.

To serve, scrape the granita off the block with a fork and spoon into Martini glasses.

Oliver!

(Carol Reed, 1968)

Oliver Twist (Mark Lester) is a cringing, two-faced little ingrate intent on fattening himself up like a prize sow on the charity of his betters. Well, maybe that's a little harsh, even if it is what the warders of his workhouse believe – but there's certainly something about twee little Oliver that brings out the savage in the people around him. Despite never having enjoyed genteel company or a proper bath, Oliver speaks in cut-glass tones and has perfectly fluffed blond locks that make him seem more like a young Prince William than a lice-ridden urchin. An orphan, he is brought up half-starving in a grim institution where the famished boys see nothing more meaty than the mutton-chop whiskers on Bumble (Harry Secombe) the beadle's Toby jug of a face. When the orphans draw lots to see who will dare to ask for more gruel, Oliver loses and is forced to quiveringly approach Mr Bumble. When he asks for more, the lardycakes who run the institution are mortified, despite the gravy-laden spittle they roar into Oliver's face containing more nutrition than he's ever eaten himself.

Thrown out as more trouble than he's worth and sold to an undertaker, angelic little Oliver soon plans his escape. Breaking out of a cellar window, he heads for the bright (candle) lights of London. But safely away from the workhouse, he can have no inkling of the adventures about to befall him in the city. Awaiting him are brushes with light-fingered cockney scamps, Jewish caricatures, murderous thugs and golden-hearted whores – and ultimately, joy in the house of a kind old man whose greatest pleasure is playing with Oliver to his heart's content.

This rather Christmassy gruel recipe is best served as a sort of sweet soup. While serving anything this rich to workhouse riffraff would be asking for trouble, you might dilute a spoon or two of it with a quart of brackish water as a reward to a deserving pauper for extra effort on the treadmill.

Fruit Gruel

75ml (3 fl oz) brandy *or* rum

50g (2 oz) pitted prunes

25g (1 oz) sultanas

4 quinces

1 tablespoon quince jelly
   (optional)

2 tablespoons soft brown sugar

1 teaspoon cinnamon

300ml (10 fl oz) milk

100g (4 oz) oats

2 tablespoons white sugar

100ml (4 fl oz) cream

Pour the brandy or rum over the prunes and sultanas and leave overnight – if you avoid buying the 'ready to eat' variety, the prunes will absorb more alcohol (surely a good thing). Peel and core the quinces and cut into chunks. Put them into a pan with just enough water to cover and add the quince jelly, if you're using it. Add the soft brown sugar and cinnamon and bring to a low simmer. After 10 minutes, stir in the dried fruit and alcohol and simmer for another 10 minutes or so, until there is very little liquid left.

Heat the milk to a low boil in a separate pan and add the oats. Boil for five minutes, until the oats are swollen and soft and the milk has thickened slightly. While it is still warm, add the white sugar to the gruel and stir until dissolved. Add the cream and stewed fruit, mix thoroughly and serve warm.

The Sound of Music

(Robert Wise, 1965)

Underneath the sugary surface of *The Sound of Music* lurks a raw, tempestuous story of lonely goatherds, angry nuns and jackbooted Nazis that too often goes unnoticed. Think about it: free and easy novice Maria Kutschera (Julie Andrews) is just too wild for her Austrian convent, so the nuns cast her out. Keen to be rid of her, the Mother Superior effectively pimps Maria to an ageing widower who, for some shadowy reason, can't keep any governesses at his house for more than five minutes. Maria's new employer, the overbearing Captain Von Trapp (Christopher Plummer), turns out to be fabulously wealthy, and Maria, recognizing a cushy meal ticket when she sees one, gets her claws into him quickly.

First she buys his children's complicity by scrapping lessons, making them new clothes and turning a blind eye when the jailbait eldest daughter runs off for steamy sessions with a local bit of Nazi rough. Then, though she's supposed to have no fleshly experience, Maria regularly dances so hard that her underwear flashes, and she even capsizes a boat full of children so she can display her breasts heaving in her tightly clinging wet bodice to the captain. This vamping soon does the trick, and Maria manages to see off Baroness Eberfeld (Doris Lloyd), the captain's rightful fiancée, pretty sharply. The baroness, after all, is no fool, and can hardly fail to notice that Maria is surrounded by a halo of soft lighting whenever she looks at the captain.

But once she's got her man, the Nazis invade and ruin everything. Forced to join the German navy or flee, the captain manages to sneak his family away from a folk concert they are singing in to escape via Maria's old convent. His daughter's old Nazi flame threatens to murder Von Trapp, and it is only because the nuns sabotage the Nazis' cars that the family are able to escape and flee the country.

We learn little of the fate of these courageous nuns, but can there be any doubt that, after their crime against the Reich, they pay for the Von Trapps' freedom with their lives? And to think this sordid, brutal tale passes for family entertainment.

Doe Schnitzels

2 tablespoons dried porcini mushrooms

4 thin venison escalopes or steaks (beef can be substituted if you can't get any venison)

2 tablespoons plain flour

2 teaspoons paprika

oil

50g (2 oz) butter

1 small onion, chopped

50g (2 oz) of pancetta (though good bacon will do)

2 sticks celery, trimmed of their strings and cubed	1 teaspoon dried thyme
	50ml (2 fl oz) beef stock
50g (2 oz) brown cap mushrooms, sliced thinly	50ml (2 fl oz) red wine
	50ml (2 fl oz) single cream

Soak the porcini in a little hot water for an hour. Beat the meat flat with a meat mallet (or a rolling pin). Mix the flour and paprika and dredge the steaks with the mixture on both sides. Fry in a little oil on both sides until well browned, then set aside. Add the butter to the pan, then the onion and pancetta, and fry gently for a few minutes until the onion has softened.

Meanwhile, remove the porcini from their water, squeeze dry (reserving the liquid), chop finely and add to the pan. Add the celery and brown cap mushrooms to the frying pan and cook two minutes longer. Then add the thyme, stock, wine and the soaking liquid from the porcini, rubbing the pan bottom with a wooden spoon as it bubbles to dislodge any meat juices dried on to it. When it has reduced by half, add the cream, simmer for a minute longer, then pour the sauce over the venison.

Sprinkle everything with the parsley and serve with buttered noodles.

Singin' in the Rain

(Stanley Donen/Gene Kelly, 1952)

Smacking the world's biggest film star in the kisser with a gateau might seem a bad start to a career on the screen, but it does the trick in putting Kathy Selden (Debbie Reynolds) on the road to fame. The chorus girl and aspiring actress commits her act of cake-based folly just after meeting silent-screen heart-throb Don Lockwood (Gene Kelly). When the actor vaults uninvited into her car to evade some crazed fans, she decides to underplay how impressed she is by affecting a lofty disdain for mere entertainment. If you've seen one film, she says, you've seen them all.

Lockwood is understandably irked: with his on-screen partner Lina Lamont (Jean Hagen), he's Hollywood's hottest property, starring in costume dramas where he compensates, by looking rather killing in tight breeches, for acting that makes the average pantomime villain seem like Laurence Olivier.

Peeved as he is, he doesn't have to wait long to see her lassoed off her high horse. Later that evening, Lockwood discovers Selden jumping out of a massive cake at a party, performing high kicks and saucy winks as part of the floor show, which is hardly the work of the serious actress she pretended to be. Furious at being found out and mocked into the bargain, Selden aims a creamy sponge at his smirking face, but misses and hits preening Lamont instead.

You'd expect this to be the last time Selden ever comes within dessert-lobbing distance of Lamont. But when the screen couple have to shoot their first talkie, Lamont has a problem that only Selden can remedy. While she looks good on celluloid, Lamont's shrill tone and Bronx honk make her sound rather like a donkey going into labour with a brace of old-school kettles coming to the boil in the same room. Kathy is called in to dub over her lines and songs – but with Lockwood in love with her, will she end up sacrificing her career to remain in Lina's shadow indefinitely?

For the authentic touch, lick this extremely rich cake off the face of the star of your choice.

Chocolate Orange Angel-food Cake

6 large eggs, separated
pinch of salt
300g (10½ oz) caster sugar
150g (5½ oz) self-raising flour

100ml (4 fl oz) orange juice
1 tablespoon candied orange
    peel, finely shredded

MUSICALS

For the filling

125g (4½ oz) softened unsalted
    butter
3 additional egg yolks
1 teaspoon candied orange peel,
    finely shredded

200g (7½ oz) icing sugar
100g (4 oz) dark chocolate
4 tablespoons water

For the sponge, beat the egg whites with the salt until they form soft peaks that just hold their shape, then gradually fold in half the caster sugar. Beat the egg yolks separately with the remaining sugar, then gradually add the flour, fruit juice and candied peel and whisk until everything is fully amalgamated. Fold the egg whites gently into the yolk mixture and spoon into two medium-sized cake tins. Bake in an oven preheated to 160°C/325°F/Mark 3 for 1 hour. Leave to cool before removing from the tin.

For the filling, beat the butter, egg yolks, peel and sugar together until smooth and creamy. Break up the chocolate and melt gently over a double boiler to which you added the water. Remove from the heat and beat in the butter mixture. Spoon half the mixture on top of one cake half and spread smoothly. Top with the other cake half and spread the remaining filling evenly on top.

Grease

(Randal Kleiser, 1978)

How old do you have to be before you get thrown out of Rydell High School? Danny Zuko (John Travolta) and the T-Birds, his gang of bad boy greasers, are just entering their senior year, but they seem so long in the tooth that they look suspiciously like cradle-snatchers smuggling themselves back into High School to grab some under-age (summer) lovin'. Thankfully, their lady-loves, such as the tough but exquisitely preserved Betty Rizzo (Stockard Channing), hardly seem any younger.

Danny has spent the school holidays at the beach with his particular squeeze, Australian hottie Sandy Olsson (Olivia Newton-John). While he's had a wild time with her, getting it on in the sand, saving her from drowning and even staying up till 10 o'clock, it has all come to an end too soon. But to his surprise, instead of returning to Australia as she was supposed to, she turns up at his school for the first day of the new term (why? – we never learn).

Although he's really pleased to see her, Danny is just too damn cool for a prim miss like Sandy. Her sensible shoes and preference for soda over alcohol sit poorly next to Danny's studded leather jacket, ostrich strut and fondness for driving round town in a souped-up pussy wagon. While they're still crazy about each other, one of them will have to change. So will Danny junk his ball-combustingly tight black jeans and transform himself into a clean-living jock? Or will Sandy learn to chew gum with her mouth open and to smoke like a proper grown-up?

Danny is seen ordering a cherry soda with chocolate ice-cream during the film, and it should be said that the unusual, deliciously retro drink that follows is most successful (excluding the alcohol) with people who haven't yet hit puberty. But as *Grease*'s cast of splendidly mature youngsters shows us, you're only as old as you feel – right?

Black Forest Ice-cream Soda

150ml (5 fl oz) chocolate milk
100ml (4 fl oz) kirschwasser
   (cherry eau de vie – optional)
roughly 300ml (10 fl oz) club
   soda or cherryade
4 scoops chocolate ice-cream
4 scoops cherry ice-cream (Ben
   & Jerry's 'Cherry Garcia'
   works very well)

4 heaped tablespoons whipped
   cream
4 tablespoons chocolate
   shavings
4 glacé cherries

Divide the chocolate milk evenly between four very tall sundae glasses. Stir in the kirschwasser if you are using it. Top up with whatever fizzy drink you have chosen, to two-thirds from the top of each glass. Carefully, put a scoop of each ice-cream into each glass. Spoon the whipped cream on top of each, then top with the chocolate shavings and a glacé cherry.

HORROR MOVIES

The Silence of the Lambs

(Jonathan Demme, 1991)

'A census-taker once tried to test me. I ate his liver with fava beans and a nice Chianti.' Dr Hannibal Lecter's (Anthony Hopkins) choice of meat might be unorthodox, but you can't fault the sound judgement of his cooking tips. He's being questioned by callow FBI rookie Clarice Starling (Jodie Foster), the fresh young meat intended to charm him into revealing what he knows about a spate of recent murders.

After indulging his penchant for human flesh too liberally, Dr Lecter has been shut up in a rather old-school dungeon in the vaults of a Baltimore mental penitentiary. Locked away behind glass and baited by his slimy nemesis Dr Chilton (Anthony Heald), Lecter's expertise as a former psychiatrist may yet prove to be the meal ticket out of his hellhole. Starling's superiors think Lecter might have clues to the identity of Buffalo Bill, a serial killer who is kidnapping, stripping and flaying women up and down the eastern sea-board. She gets surprisingly matey with the perversely charming Lecter, whose waspish appraisal of her perfume and accessories takes her aback. He, in turn, starts drawing mooning pictures of her cradling lambs, hoping perhaps to produce art so mawkishly twee that his jailers are too busy laughing to keep tabs on him.

Meanwhile, Buffalo Bill has culled another victim, senator's daughter Catherine Martin (Brooke Smith), and generously put her on his own invented regime for shedding the pounds – he imprisons her down a well and feeds her on scraps. But why does he need her thin? And how much longer does Agent Starling have to tease his motives and whereabouts out of Lecter?

He has been leading her slowly to the harrowing conclusion that things are considerably worse than they imagined. Buffalo Bill is not merely a cold-hearted psychopath; he might even be – oh, horror! – a transvestite to boot. Knowing that nothing in America can be deemed sacred while there's a man in women's undies on the loose, the FBI start a frantic scramble for the killer. But when Lecter scalps and disembowels his way out of prison armed only with a microscopic piece of tin, it's far from clear who is going to be for dinner next – Dr Chilton, Catherine Martin, Buffalo Bill, or Agent Starling herself.

True to form, Dr Lecter's pairing of liver, fava beans and Chianti is restrained and tasteful in everything except the origin of its ingredients. This recipe extends the classic *Fegato alla Veneziana* by adding beans and pancetta. Though the onions require slow cooking, it's otherwise an extremely simple dish to rustle up whenever you fancy having an old friend for dinner – and (I'm sorry, I can't resist) it won't cost you an arm and a leg, either.

Liver with Fava Beans and Chianti

6 medium onions	20g (¾ oz) butter
4 tablespoons olive oil	salt and pepper
2 cloves garlic, chopped	1 tablespoon chopped flat-leaf
500g (18 oz) broad (aka fava)	parsley
beans	2 tablespoons Chianti or other
100g (4 oz) diced pancetta	red wine
400g (14 oz) calves' liver	2 tablespoons red wine vinegar

Halve the onions and slice into thin strands. Heat half of the oil in a frying pan, then add the onions and garlic and cook over a very low heat until they are very soft. This takes around 45 minutes, so you must keep the heat low, stir them occasionally and make sure they do not crisp. While they are cooking, shell the broad beans. If any are especially large, scratch the skin with a knife and peel them. Boil in water until tender, usually about 15 minutes. Heat the rest of the oil in a second pan and fry the pancetta over high heat until crisp. Remove to kitchen paper and leave to drain thoroughly.

Slice the liver into thin strands. Once the onions are cooked, remove them from the pan and melt the butter, but don't wash the pan yet. Season the strips of liver and fry in the onion pan briefly over high heat for about 45 seconds, then transfer to a colander and drain. Mix the pancetta, parsley and onions together in a serving dish and place the liver on top. Add the wine and vinegar to the frying pan and boil down to half its volume, scraping the pan bottom with a wooden spoon to dislodge any dried-on juices. Pour over the liver and serve immediately.

As this dish is rather rich, it goes well with a glass of the Chianti you cooked it with as well as a plain accompaniment, such as mashed potatoes, followed by a green salad.

Rosemary's Baby

(Roman Polanski, 1968)

Put yourself in poor Rosemary Woodhouse's (Mia Farrow) shoes. One minute she's having dinner with her actor husband Guy (John Cassavetes), looking forward to starting a family, the next she's semi-conscious and being ravished by the anti-Christ, surrounded by a coven of what look like naked dinner ladies. No wonder she spends the rest of the film mooching around like a drowned puppy who's discovered Vidal Sassoon.

Rosemary's slide from wholesome housewife to writhing devil's wench began just a few weeks back, when she and Guy moved into the Bramford building. Although it seems to be inhabited mainly by thickly bespectacled old dears, this ominous neo-Gothic pile off New York's Central Park has a lurid reputation as the former haunt of occultists and cannibals. Sure enough, almost as soon as they arrive, an apparently cheerful young woman who Rosemary befriends in the laundry room jumps from a high window to her death.

This puts the Woodhouses in touch with the girl's grieving protectors, their elderly neighbours the Castevets. The charming Minnie Castevet (Ruth Gordon) has a fondness for snooping and a taste in clothes that makes her look like an exceptionally florid lamp stand. She pressures the

Woodhouses into coming round for dinner to meet her husband Roman (Sidney Blackmer), where they overload them with indigestible steak and some tell-tale grumblings about the hypocrisy of organized religion (people who dislike the Pope are usually devil-worshippers, I find). Rosemary is bored silly, but when her shifty husband senses that the Castevets might be able to help his stalled acting career, he agrees to go back alone the following night.

Soon after, Guy's career suddenly takes off when a rival actor is stricken blind and he lands the role. Delighted with his success, Guy and Rosemary enjoy a quiet meal at home together, with desserts provided from next door by Minnie Castevet. But is there something wrong with Rosemary's chocolate mousse? Doesn't it have a 'chalky undertaste', she wonders? Whatever the mousse contains, the next thing she knows, she's in bed, next door's Satanists are chanting all around her and a furry paw is stroking her tender flesh. Though she doesn't remember her night spent rutting with her demoniacal hot rod, she soon falls pregnant – but can she look forward to a cute little Rosemary Jnr, or does she have a tiger in her tank?

With *Rosemary's Baby*, the old cliché about rich desserts being wicked rings true for once. This recipe is free of sleeping pills and witchy tannis root, but has the added option of crushed-up Rennies if you want to replicate the chalkiness of the original. Crème de menthe can be bought in small bottles, but if you prefer not to shell out, a few drops of peppermint essence will add the necessary mintiness.

Chalky Mint Chocolate Mousse

120g (4½ oz) best quality bitter
    chocolate (such as Valrhona)
2 tablespoons crème de menthe
2 tablespoons double cream
4 eggs

80g (3 oz) icing sugar
2 spearmint Rennies (optional)
pinch of salt
fresh mint leaves to garnish

Break up the chocolate and put into a bowl. Rest this bowl over a pan of gently boiling water and melt. Stir in the crème de menthe and cream and leave to cool. Separate the eggs. Sieve the icing sugar into the yolks, beat this in firmly and then add to the chocolate. If using them, crush the Rennies in a mortar, then stir into the chocolate. Add the salt to the egg whites and whisk them until they are stiff. Fold the whites gently into the chocolate mixture, taking care not to deflate the mousse by stirring too hard.

Turn the mixture into four china ramekins (or similar small, straight-sided china bowls) and leave in the fridge for at least four hours before serving, garnished with the mint.

Scream

(Wes Craven, 1996)

One night, you find yourself alone in a large dark house somewhere out of town. You are snuggled up on the sofa with a bowl of popcorn and a DVD of your favourite film (*Driller Killer*, or maybe *Cannibal Dawn*), when a grunt-voiced psychopath calls you and tells you you're going to die. Outside you can hear a strange whirring and a flurry of bodies in the murk. Could there be a camera crew out there waiting to catch your final agonizing death throes in lurid colour? If so, what should you do?

Wes Craven's *Scream* thrashes out these basic rules for surviving a horror movie:

1 Underneath the scary masks, psychopaths are mostly prim conservatives who loathe seeing teenagers enjoy themselves; so have sex in a slasher film and you'll soon find yourself carved up like a Thanksgiving turkey.

2 Not only do psychos disapprove of anything beyond heavy petting, they're generally the sort of clean-living folk who believe that drugs and alcohol are not the way forward for tomorrow's youth – so, kids, if you don't want to end up crucified upside down on a telegraph pole, just say no.

3 No one likes a know-it-all, so never say 'I'll be right back' before slipping out for five minutes. Being too cocksure about returning from an errand alive is the sort of arrogance that makes your average slasher see red – if you haven't checked your back porch for machete-wielding scalp hunters waiting to carve their initials in your tender flesh, how can you be so certain?

4 Don't ask 'Who's there?' It's the killer, you idiot! Otherwise they would have told you already.

5 Never, ever go out to investigate a strange noise. What on earth are you trying to prove? If it's just foxes humping on the back lawn then leave them to it, and if it's the groans of an escaped mental patient teasing someone's kidneys out of their carcase with a skewer, do you really need to see it close up?

Unfortunately, many of *Scream*'s characters are negligent of these rules, so when a hooded killer masked as a yawning skull appears in their midst, most of them end up tripping over their own insides as they try to flee his gore-streaked blade. But will the standard-issue virgin heroine Sidney Prescott (Neve Campbell) be able to escape his wrath? Of course she will – rule number 6 is that the heroine always survives, even if the killer can't be guaranteed to be completely dead . . .

In *Scream*, popcorn is the last meal that the killer's first victim (Drew Barrymore) prepares herself, and this simple but moreish recipe is probably my favourite way of making it. Not only does the nutmeg add an interesting undertone to the richness of the raspberry jam, the scarlet colour prevents your snack being spoiled if one of your party gets spiked like a squealing piggy before your very eyes and spatters it with blood.

Bloody Popcorn

70g (2½ oz) butter	5 tablespoons raspberry jam
200g (7½ oz) popcorn	¼ teaspoon grated nutmeg
3 tablespoons soft brown sugar	

Melt a tiny bit of the butter in a large pan and pour in the popcorn. Shake the pan to coat all of the grains, then leave over a gentle heat until the grains have popped. Transfer the corn to a baking dish, taking care not to take any remaining unpopped grains at the bottom of the pan. Melt the rest of the butter in a small pan and stir in the sugar, jam and nutmeg, stirring vigorously over a low heat to help dissolve the sugar. Pour this all over the corn and stir to coat it thoroughly. Place the popcorn in an oven preheated to 200°C/400°F/Mark 6 and bake for 10 minutes (this helps fix the coating).

Remove from the oven and leave to cool and harden before eating. Once it's cool, the popcorn may need breaking up into pieces, but stays separate from then onwards.

The Exorcist

(William Friedkin, 1973)

There's no accounting for the rush of teenage hormones. At the beginning of *The Exorcist*, Regan MacNeil (Linda Blair) is a sweet, innocent girl whose tender bud of womanhood is just beginning to unfurl. Within barely a week, she's a screeching, foul-mouthed harpy swearing like a drunken sailor, jabbing her rude bits with a crucifix and painting comedy knockers on statues of the Virgin Mary. This may sound like pretty normal pubescent behaviour nowadays, but *The Exorcist* comes from a more innocent time when a teenager uttering naughty words could only be explained away by demonic possession.

While her mother, the famous actress Claire MacNeil (Ellen Burstyn), is shooting a film on the Georgetown campus, Regan whiles away her days dreaming of getting a horse and chatting away with her imaginary friend, Captain Howdy. Evidently, he's no longer good company, for she suddenly starts making things up and spewing obscenities. Deciding heavy intervention is the only way to curb Regan's new outspokenness, doctors prescribe the usual treatment for any troubled child who starts speaking their mind: oodles of Ritalin. Unsurprisingly, it fails – though she does develop an impressive ability to walk like a spider and swivel her neck, so the treatment is not entirely without dividends. When the drug cabinet fails to stop Regan's degeneration, her desperate mother reaches for the Bible, calling in Father Damien Karras (Jason Miller), an anguished priest-cum-psychiatrist still reeling with guilt after the death of his lonely mother.

Clair MacNeil now believes there's a demon in her daughter, but Karras is only slowly persuaded that anything more than a case of raging hormones is responsible for Regan's flip. Turning up with the good book and a holster full of holy water, he starts bantering with the spirit inside the girl's body. In one of the film's more memorable lines, this spirit informs Father Karras that his deceased mother is engaging in uncharacteristic sensual abandon somewhere beyond this mortal world (and it isn't heaven). With this much obscenity flying around, the Church decides it's time to send in their biggest gun, arch-exorcist Father Lankester Merrin (Max von Sydow). This might seem excessive pressure merely to cool a teenager's growing-pains, but as Regan starts bringing up her dinner in funny colours and levitating, Father Merrin sees beyond her look-at-me antics and starts to recognize the work of an old, formidable demon adversary.

The emission brought forth by Regan in the film is actually pea soup – not the most appealing culinary accompaniment to any scene of ritual vomiting. A far better look-alike substitute is this sharp, intensely flavoured dessert cocktail, which is so refreshing that you'd eat it even if it came gurgling out of Regan's twisted mouth. Maybe.

Gin- and Lime-flavoured Demon Bile

10 limes	20g (¾ oz) gelatine
2 clementines	200ml (7 fl oz) dry gin
200ml (7 fl oz) water	¼ teaspoon (8 drops) green food
200g (7½ oz) granulated sugar	colouring

Remove the zest of 1 of the limes and cut into superfine shreds. Squeeze the limes' and clementines' juice into a bowl. Measure out the water and heat in a pan over a low flame. Add the sugar and lime zest and bring gently to the boil, stirring all the while. When the sugar is fully dissolved, remove from the heat and leave to cool. While it is still hot, fill a teacup with a small amount of this liquid. Sprinkle the gelatine on top and whip vigorously with a fork until it is fully absorbed. If the liquid cools too quickly to absorb the gelatine, stand it in a pan partly filled with hot water and stir again. Pour the fruit juice, gin, green food colouring, partially cooled syrup and gelatine emulsion into a 1 litre (35 fl oz) mould. Mix carefully and leave to set.

You could feasibly leave this to set fully and then turn it out, but I like it best after about 6 hours in the fridge when it's a semi-gelatinous gloop, so that you can spoon solid lumps still swimming in demon bile into waiting chilled serving glasses. Eat with a spoon.

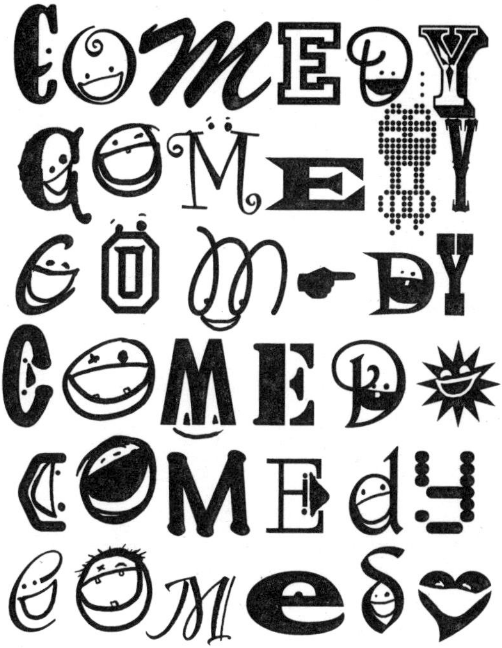

Monty Python's Life of Brian

(Terry Jones, 1979)

'He's not the Messiah! He's a very naughty boy!' says Brian Cohen's mother (Terry Jones) to the multitudes assembled beneath the balcony of their Jerusalem hovel. A nonentity who scrapes a living hawking otters' noses in the town's arena, her son (Graham Chapman) has been mistaken by the rabble for God's emissary. Hiding among a motley line-up of hectoring false prophets to escape a Roman patrol one day, Brian accidentally finds himself hailed as God reborn by a demented mob.

You can sort of see his followers' point, though: while Brian isn't the Son of God, he was given birth to by what appears to be a man in drag, so he is surely a miracle of sorts.

Born in the stable next to Jesus's, Brian has been close to greatness ever since the three kings got the wrong address and almost landed his grumbling mother with gifts of sparkling gold, exquisite frankincense and utterly useless myrrh. It's not until he becomes embroiled with the People's Front of Judea, however, that his unwelcome fame starts to grow. An anti-Roman collective of self-governing anarcho-syndicalists, the PFJ are the sort of rebels who, come the revolution, would be swanning around party headquarters with clipboards while the rest of us did the work. As they loathe the Romans almost as much as their enemies, the Judean People's Front, they press Brian to accept a mission that is wildly dangerous but vital to the survival of their cause: daubing a little graffiti on some public buildings. His success so impresses the PFJ that it gets him into the loincloth of strident revolutionary Judith (Sue Jones-Davies). When he wakes up in bed with her one morning, however, the crowds he finds clamouring outside his balcony are hoping for a second coming of an altogether different sort.

Thus unfolds a satire on cult followers that does its best to offend the adherents of just about every religion. When Brian's acolytes are not abasing themselves beneath his holy sandal or persecuting non-believers, they are reeling from his great miracle – casually pointing out a juniper bush that just happens to have some vaguely nourishing berries on it. The requisite persecution that will complete his messianic status comes soon after, when he is sentenced to crucifixion – but can fruity Pontius Pilate's (Michael Palin) speech impediment save him from the excruciating martyrdom his revolutionary colleagues so devoutly wish for?

This Levantine recipe commemorates the little walk-on part Jesus has in the film, when we watch his followers jostle and squabble at the back of the crowd at the Sermon on the Mount. The number of ingredients might seem small, but you'll be surprised – a little goes a long way.

Loaves and Fishes

For the loaves

2 teaspoons dried yeast
6 tablespoons warm water
150g (5½ oz) plain yoghurt
½ teaspoon bicarbonate of soda

150g (5½ oz) barley flour
120g (4½ oz) wholemeal wheat
flour
½ teaspoon salt

For the fishes

1 tablespoon ground cumin
1 small red chilli, roughly
chopped
2 heaped tablespoons chopped
flat-leaf parsley
4 cloves garlic
1 tablespoon lemon juice
6 tablespoons olive oil

1.5kg (3½ lb) whole fish such as
red snapper, cleaned and
scaled
1 onion, chopped
100g (4 oz) green olives, pitted
and halved
tahini (sesame seed paste –
optional)

Prepare the bread well in advance, as there are two proofing
stages. Dissolve the yeast in the water. In a separate bowl, mix the
yoghurt and the bicarbonate of soda until it foams. Sieve the flours
into the bowl, add the salt, and mix with the yoghurt and yeast.
Form into a dough, adding an extra tablespoon of water if you
have trouble getting it to cohere. Knead the dough vigorously for
15 minutes. Cover the bowl with a damp cloth and leave somewhere warm to rise for 90 minutes.

For the fish, put the herbs, spices, garlic, lemon juice and half the oil in a blender and blend to a fine paste. Rub this into the fish and leave to marinate for 30 minutes. Meanwhile, cook the onion in a little more of the olive oil until translucent. Put the fish in a baking dish and surround with the olives and onion. Drizzle the rest of the oil on top. Cover the whole dish in foil and bake in an oven preheated to 200°C/400°F/Mark 6 for 40 minutes, basting at least twice during the cooking.

While the fish is in the oven, return to the bread. Turn the dough on to a floured board and divide it into 8 portions. Make each into a ball, then into a thin disc roughly the size of your handspan. Cover and leave for a further 20 minutes. Heat a large flat frying pan to a medium-high heat with a dribble of olive oil. Put one dough disc into the pan and cook for two minutes. Turn over and cook another minute. Do the same with the other 7, then wrap in a cloth so that you can eat them while still warm. Serve with the fish, some extra flat-leaf parsley, and tahini to dribble on top.

Serves five thousand.

This Is Spinal Tap

(Rob Reiner, 1984)

'There's a fine line between clever and . . . stupid,' remarks Spinal Tap's lead singer David St Hubbins (Michael McKean). Apparently the line is too fine for the fading, Spandex-clad cock-rockers' perceptions, as the British band consistently trip over it while touring the United States in a desperate attempt to avoid complete career oblivion.

For starters, they are bemused when the record company deems the cover of their new album *Smell the Glove* sexist, even though it features a naked woman on a leash with a glove being forced into her mouth. Then when they commission a mock-up of Stonehenge to liven up their stage show, they accidentally order it only 18 inches (45 cm) high, leaving it in grave danger of being crushed by the dwarf paid to dance around it. As if those errors of judgement weren't killing enough, lead guitarist Nigel Tufnel (Christopher Guest) has to contend with substandard backstage catering. 'How can anyone make a sandwich with miniature bread?' he asks long-suffering manager Ian Faith (Tony Hendra), trying to fold a normal-sized slice over a tiny piece of ham – and why does one of the (pimento-stuffed) olives 'have a little guy in it'?

Thankfully, Tufnel is a true professional and refuses to let the backstage nibbles fiasco affect his performance. After all, their career has already had its fair share of tragedy. Not only was their previous album *Shark Sandwich* dubbed 'Shit Sandwich' by the critics, a string of their drummers have died – from a bizarre gardening accident, choking on someone else's vomit and spontaneous human combustion respectively. Still this hasn't held them back – though it might explain the note of pathos in Tufnel's haunting piano ballad 'Lick My Love Pump'. But when St Hubbins's meddling girlfriend Jeanine (June Chadwick) ousts Faith as manager and decides that horoscopes are more important than the proper planning of the band's stairway to rock heaven, it looks like the Tap's final countdown might be just around the corner.

While his knack of capturing Nigel Tufnel's mockney suburban drawl is little short of miraculous, Christopher Guest actually became the 5th Baron Haden-Guest of Saling in 1996. Accordingly, this is a considerably posher, traditionally English version of the basic ham-and-bread combo Tufnel had to make do with backstage. If you can't be bothered baking the gammon, the sauce is still one of the best accompaniments to pork or ham you can find; on a scale of one to ten, it goes up to – you guessed it – eleven.

Roast Gammon Sandwiches
with Cumberland Sauce

1.5kg (3½ lb) gammon joint
2 bay leaves
1 handful cloves

2 tablespoons clear honey
½ tablespoon black pepper

For the sauce

zest of 2 oranges
4 tablespoons redcurrant jelly
2 teaspoons orange juice

2 teaspoons dry mustard
salt and pepper
10ml (2 teaspoons) port

Also

bread
butter

radishes

Soak the gammon in cold water for 24 hours. Drain and rinse thoroughly. Put the gammon in a pan and cover with more water. Add the bay leaves and gently simmer for 1 hour. Drain and pat the gammon dry with kitchen paper. Score the fat on the gammon into a deep diamond pattern with a sharp knife and stud a corner of each diamond with a clove. Blend the honey with the pepper and rub energetically into the fat. Bake in an oven preheated to 200°C/400°F/Mark 6 for 45 minutes.

While the gammon is baking, make the sauce. Slice the orange zest into thin slivers and boil in a little water for 5 minutes. Fill a medium-sized saucepan a third of the way up with water and bring to the boil on a low heat. Strain the zest out of its cooking liquid and place in a china bowl. Balance this bowl over the simmering saucepan, so that the contents can cook gently over the steam. Add the redcurrant jelly, orange juice, mustard and seasoning and stir until the jelly dissolves. Stir in the port and cook for 5 further minutes. Remove from the heat and leave to solidify.

Spread liberally over slices of gammon to make sandwiches, adding some crunch with a garnish of thinly sliced radishes.

Serves 5–6.

Carry on Camping

(Gerald Thomas, 1969)

Love-starved bachelors Sid Boggle (Sid James) and Bernie Lugg (Bernard Bresslaw) are constantly scheming to get their girlfriends to play around with them, but they never quite pull it off. The women in question, Joan Fussey (Joan Sims) and Anthea Meeks (Dilys Laye), are the sort of proper young(ish) ladies who still live with Mother and only swear when it slips out, so Sid and Bernie reckon that maybe a change of scene might help loosen their corsets a notch. They hit on an idea: why not invite the girls away for a holiday, then take them unsuspectingly to nudie Camp Paradise?

Unfortunately, the campsite proves to be a muddy field where everybody is fully clothed, and the only fiddling going on is by the site's shifty, money-grabbing owner, Mr Fiddler (Peter Butterworth). Not only do the women refuse to share a tent with them, it starts to rain when Sid and Bernie try to pitch theirs and, as men often do, they have all sorts of trouble getting it up under water. They're not the only unhappy campers on site. Even though he hates cycling, Poor Mr Potter (Terry Scott) next door has had to straddle a tandem all the way there – and with such a domineering horsey wife, it's no wonder he loathes getting his leg over. He arrives at Camp Paradise looking saddle-sore and uncomfortable, which is hardly surprising as he's come in his shorts.

Still, all is not lost. When a coach party from the Chayste Place finishing school for young ladies turns up, the poor men's blood comes rushing back and their spirits rise to full height once more. Sadly, the (exceedingly mature) girls are not unchaperoned. Their head teacher Dr Soaper (Kenneth Williams) has come along, bringing the school's buxom gym mistress Miss Haggard (Hattie Jacques), who is unwilling to have her girls exposed alone to thorns, nettles and other hazards of life in the raw, knowing full well that even a little prick can cause quite a swelling. Things hot up at last when the girls attempt a little group gymnastics. When minx Babs (Barbara Windsor) flings her arms too wide, her bikini top catapults halfway across the field. The girls seem keen for a tumble, but how can Sid and Bernie evade girlfriends and teachers to find a moment to slip into Babs?

These crumpets make a good match for the innocently naughty delights of *Carry On Camping*. The only hurdle is that they need to be cooked in special metal rings (see p. 265), but if you don't have any, you can try cooking them in high-sided metal biscuit-cutters. Even if you're not endowed with the necessary equipment, the saucy accompaniment detailed here still makes a delicious, easy alternative to home-made jam, either with shop-bought crumpets or spread over a nice big pair of baps.

COMEDY

Saucy Crumpet

350g (12 oz) unbleached plain
    flour
large pinch of salt

400ml (14 fl oz) milk
1 tablespoon dried yeast
pinch of sugar

For the fruit sauce

200g (7½ oz) dried figs, ready to
    eat or pre-soaked in water
100g (4 oz) dried apricots, ready
    to eat or pre-soaked
juice and zest of 1 lemon
150ml (5 fl oz) freshly squeezed
    orange juice

1 tablespoon clear honey
1 teaspoon ground cinnamon
¼ teaspoon grated nutmeg
butter

Plus

crumpet rings × 4

Sieve the flour and salt into a bowl. Warm a quarter of the milk and mix it with the yeast in a cup. Sprinkle the sugar on top and leave for ten minutes, until foam has formed on top. Warm the rest of the milk. Pour the yeasty milk into a well in the centre of the flour, then add the remaining milk. Stir with a wooden spoon, lifting it high to beat in the milk as you go, until you have a smooth, fully amalgamated batter. Cover with a cloth and leave in a warm place to rise for 45 minutes.

Meanwhile, make your fruit sauce. Chop the figs and apricots into little cubes (this can be done in a blender, but don't mush them). Slice the lemon zest into thin strands. Heat the orange and lemon juice and the honey in a pan until simmering, then add the fruit, zest and spices. Bring to the boil and cook gently for 15 minutes, stirring every 30 seconds or so. Add water if it looks in danger of sticking. By the end, the fruit should be tender but with a modicum of bite remaining, and bonded in a thick, gooey but not runny, sauce. Spoon into a bowl or jar and leave to cool.

Grease your crumpet rings with butter (you don't have to use these, but if you don't your crumpets will come out more like flat dropped scones than traditional high-sided cakes). Heat a large frying pan to medium heat, also with a little butter, and put in the crumpet rings. Spoon 2 tablespoons of batter into each ring and cook for 5 minutes, until the surface is bubbly and slightly golden. Remove the rings, flip over the crumpets and cook a further two minutes on the other side. Repeat the process until all the batter has gone.

Toast the crumpets again briefly before serving them with butter and the fruit sauce.

Alien

(Ridley Scott, 1979)

Men giving birth to monsters, vulnerable astronauts edging down dark, slimy tunnels, a horrific egg-laying opponent whose drooling mouth is lined with fangs, and an evil computer called Mother – Freud would have a field day watching *Alien* (that is, if he was brave enough to come out from behind the sofa). A classic slab of sci-fi body horror, the film boasts more gunk and ooze than a vat of KY Jelly and more orifices, both human and mechanical, than a hospital colonoscopy department.

As the curtain rises, the crew of the commercial spaceship *Nostromo* are hauling a massive load of mineral ore back to earth, when they receive a distress signal from a nearby planet. Following the orders of their company-controlled computer, the crew land on the planet to investigate. A search party goes out into the bleak, windswept terrain outside the ship (a sort of rocky version of the Isle of Sheppey) and discovers a ruined spacecraft, derelict and abandoned in the howling wastes. As everyone watching inwardly screams 'Don't go in there!', the crew enter the ship's dark heart, a huge chamber filled with what look like Easter eggs made of jelly. But instead of disgorging a bag of sugary treats, one of the pods vomits out a hideous creature – the bastard love child of an octopus and a crab – which attaches itself to the face of crew member Kane (John Hurt).

With the creature sucking Kane's face as if it were an exceptionally juicy boiled sweet, the search team bundles him back to the ship. Against the orders of the second-in-command, Ellen Ripley (Sigourney Weaver), who fears a quarantine violation, the crew's science officer Ash (Ian Holm) lets the search party re-enter the craft. Mercifully, the creature loosens its grip on Kane's face and dies after a day, allowing Kane to wake from his coma. But just as the crew are enjoying a dinner to celebrate his recovery, a sharp-toothed phallic worm rips its way out of Kane's belly like a Jack-in-the-box and scuttles out into the ship's murky depths. With only six crew members left and an unspeakable crawling, hissing death machine skulking around their craft's nooks and crannies, can the terrified humans on board keep their cool long enough to squish the evil critter before it violates every last one of them with its slimy protuberances?

This recipe is a variant on an hors d'oeuvre popular in Scandinavia, and celebrates the alien's wonderful reproductive ingenuity – a dish of eggs, stuffed with eggs. If I were you, I'd eat them early on in your viewing of the film – while the thought of providing a host for the seedpods of another life form hasn't yet entirely lost its appeal.

Note The recipe provides more rémoulade sauce than you will actually need to stuff the eggs, so that you don't end up throwing away any hard-boiled yolks (extra whites, after all, are easier to deal with, as they can quickly and simply be turned into meringue), and it will keep a couple of days in the fridge. In France, rémoulade sauce is most popularly combined with thin julienne strips of celeriac to make a salad, an excellent way of using up any left over from this dish.

Devilled Eggs with Lumpfish Caviare

6 large eggs

3 teaspoons wine vinegar

3 extra egg yolks

pepper

2 teaspoons wholegrain mustard

360ml (12 fl oz) good olive oil

1 heaped tablespoon chives

1 heaped tablespoon tarragon

2 teaspoons capers

12 teaspoons lumpfish caviar

lettuce leaves for serving

Boil the eggs until hard – about 8 minutes. Plunge into cold water, and once they are cool enough to handle, peel off their shells. Slice each egg in half lengthwise.

For the rémoulade sauce, carefully scoop out the yolk from each one with a spoon. Put these yolks in a large mixing bowl, add one and a half teaspoons of the vinegar and pound into a paste with a wooden spoon or pestle. Add the extra yolks (raw), the pepper and the mustard and mix well (as the caviar and capers are rather salty, no extra salt is required). Start pouring in the oil drop by drop, beating the mixture with a spoon as you do.

Gradually increase the quantities of oil, beating all the time. When the oil is half used up, beat in the remaining vinegar. Keep on beating until all the oil is added and you have a thick fluffy mixture. This process can also be carried out in a food mixer if you have one. Chop the herbs and capers finely and stir into your sauce.

Carefully fill the cavities in your hard-boiled eggs with the sauce (some chefs use a piping bag for this, but I find life is too short for such complications). When you have done this, top each egg with a generous teaspoonful of the caviar, and garnish with a few extra chopped chives.

Serve on a bed of lettuce leaves, as a starter.

Star Wars Episode IV:
A New Hope

(George Lucas, 1977)

Ignore the 'Episode IV' nonsense – no amount of dodgy prequels can conceal the fact that this is the original *Star Wars* film, where we meet the cast of noble Jedi Knights, man-sized monkeys, pantomime villains and bickering robots for the first time.

As the series begins, much of the universe is suffering under the tyranny of a cruel and exploitative regime known simply as 'the Empire'. While this force of darkness keeps a whole galaxy in its vice-like grip, a small band of right-thinking terrorists – I mean rebels – are doing their best to blow the Empire's ambitions sky high. Unfortunately, they suffer a huge setback when Imperial troops intercept a rebel leader, earmuff-hairstyled Princess Leia (Carrie Fisher), carrying blueprints showing how the Empire's massive space centre and intergalactic murder pod, the Death Star, can be destroyed. The princess is imprisoned by metallic Imperial powermonger Darth Vader (David Prowse), a fireman's-helmet-wearing heavy breather who appears to have a car ashtray strapped on to his face.

Vader has her tortured, but all in vain, as the princess has wisely entrusted the blueprints to her two faithful androids: fussy fruit loop C-3PO (Anthony Daniels) and lovable trolley

R2-D2 (Kenny Baker). The pair flee Leia's ship in an escape pod and land on the surface of desolate Tatooine. The planet proves to be a futuristic version of the Old West where manly all-American pioneers are taming the wild frontier – except that, instead of fighting off war-painted Apache they're fending off bands of screeching, masked rodents. The two trusty 'droids in due course cross paths with Luke Skywalker (Mark Hamill), who shows interest in them only when R2-D2 transmits a distress signal intended for someone called Obi-Wan Kenobi. Luke is intrigued: could he be referring to the old bearded loon Ben Kenobi (Alec Guinness) living all alone out in Injun country?

Through all this, Luke will come into contact with the Jedi, a rather spooky troupe of telepathic warrior-monks destined to lord it over the rest of the universe through the use of an intuitive power called 'the Force'. This Force supposedly exhorts them to preserve peace and freedom throughout the universe. In the film, however, it seems to be mainly useful for the noble purpose of screwing with Imperial troopers' minds, or killing things when your eyes are closed. Although Luke is reluctant at first, he eventually pursues his true calling: taking part in a huge video game where he gets to slaughter loads of people in masks and attack enemies with what appears to be a really cool-looking disco light.

This dish reflects the severely limited range of food available on Luke Skywalker's home planet of Tatooine. As any *Star Wars* fan will know, outside the moisture farms the only wild food the planet produces in any abundance is mushrooms, which thrive in the lush humidity of the farms' ventilation vents (or so I'm told). The coriander seeds in the mushrooms' dipping sauce are a nod to the spice trade, apparently so essential to the galactic economy.

Tatooine Mushroom Skewers

150g (5½ oz) chestnut
  mushrooms
150g (5½ oz) shiitake
  mushrooms

6 tablespoons olive oil
juice of half a lemon

For the dipping sauce

6 tomatoes
2 cloves garlic, finely chopped
6 tablespoons water
¼ teaspoon thyme

¼ teaspoon coriander seeds
1 bay leaf
dash of black pepper

Plus

4–6 long skewers

Rub the mushrooms clean with a damp cloth or kitchen towel. Toss them in 4 tablespoons of the olive oil and all the lemon juice and leave to marinate for a couple of hours. Remove the mush-rooms and thread on the skewers.

Scratch a little cross in the skin of each tomato and cover them with boiling water. After 30 seconds, drain them, peel off the now loosened skins and chop finely. Heat the remaining olive oil in a pan, along with anything that is left of the mushrooms' marinade. Fry the garlic briefly in it over medium heat until it is just turning brown. Add the chopped tomatoes, water, thyme, coriander seeds, bay leaf and pepper and bring to a gentle boil. Cook for 15 minutes, or until the tomatoes have largely disintegrated into the sauce and most of the water has boiled off. While the sauce is cooking, grill the mushrooms for 5 minutes, in a pan lined with foil, turning them once.

Take from the grill and serve as a starter, with the sauce (minus the bay leaf) to dip the mushrooms in. This dish is also good as an accompaniment to grilled trout.

Soylent Green

(Richard Fleischer, 1973)

Cities of forty million inhabitants, a greenhouse effect turning the world into a sauna, overprocessed junk food that tastes of nothing. So many features of *Soylent Green* have come true you might at times think it was an extremely depressing documentary. Then you notice the mushroom-cloud afros, creaking sexual politics and slack-jawed awe with which a clunky 'Space Invaders' game is paraded, and remember with relief that you're safely back in the realms of early 70s melodrama.

The film is set in 2022 in a sprawling, sultry New York, where huge hordes of the unemployed have congregated and resources are so scarce that people are mugged for their water ration (it could almost be Glastonbury). 'Crazy scientists' (could this be the world's most unjustly maligned profession?) have turned the land into arid waste and the oceans into brackish sewers through industrial pollution, and 'real' food is so scarce that a jar of strawberries costs more than a man's life. The ragged populace is dependent on the artificial Frankenstein foods made by the shadowy Soylent Corporation, of which the most prized is Soylent Green, an unappealing lozenge that looks like a form of vinyl tiling.

Swaggering his way through this nightmare cityscape is

Detective Robert Thorn (Charlton Heston), a gung-ho maverick who would no doubt be mortified to learn that his slanted cap and nattily tied bandana make him look rather fruity (not that much fruit is to be had in *Soylent Green*). He's sent to investigate the murder of bigwig lawyer William R. Simonson (Joseph Cotten) at the exclusive Chelsea Towers, a top-security high-rise blessed with luxuries such as hot running water and scraggy bits of old celery on sale in its shop. There he meets Shirl (Leigh Taylor-Young), the dead man's 'furniture' – that is, a sexual and domestic underling that came with the rental on his apartment. Simonson's murder appears to have been the accompaniment to a random burglary, but both Thorn and the depressingly passive Shirl suspect foul play. When Thorn discovers Simonson's link to the Soylent Corporation, the powers that be do what they can to get him off the job. But before they succeed, Thorn learns some unpalatable truths about the source of Soylent's mystery wonder food.

As you'd expect, this recipe for Soylent Green looks very much like its counterpart in the film, but excludes some of the foodstuff's less appetizing ingredients (though I suppose you could add them if you really wanted to).

SCIENCE FICTION

Soylent Green Halva Macaroon Squares

150g (5½ oz) shelled unsalted
   pistachio nuts
150g peeled (or ready-ground)
   almonds
100g (4 oz) granulated sugar

8 drops green food colouring
   (desirable, but not essential,
   as the pistachios are greenish)
150ml (5 fl oz) milk
20g (¾ oz) unsalted butter

Plus

greaseproof paper

rice paper

Note If you find rice paper tricky to get hold of, then use a buttered sheet of greaseproof paper instead – but beware, the macaroon squares are rather sticky.

Put the nuts in a blender (just the pistachios if your almonds are pre-ground) and pulse to a fine powder. You will find that you have to stop during this process and poke out nuts which have stuck to the blade, as their natural oiliness makes them rather sticky. When they are fully ground, mix the nuts with the sugar. Add any food colouring you are using to the milk and stir this into the nuts to make a paste. Melt the butter in a pan over a medium flame and add the nut paste. Stirring constantly, let it thicken and cook for 5–7 minutes. The mixture is ready when it's starting to come away from the sides as one lump.

   Line a baking tin with the greaseproof paper, cover its bottom with a sheet of rice paper, then spoon the mixture over it. Using the most flat-bladed knife you have, smooth the paste to about half a centimetre's thickness (about as thick as the tip of your little finger). Bake in an oven preheated to 150°C/300°F/Mark 2 for half an hour. Remove from the oven and leave to cool completely before slicing right through the rice paper to create a grid of 2cm (¾ inch) squares.

Serve with Turkish coffee or fresh mint tea.

Casablanca

(Michael Curtiz, 1942)

How does Ilsa Lund (Ingrid Bergman) keep it up? Despite having been in hiding from the Nazis for months, she enters Rick's Café Américain looking every bit like she has just strolled in from a mildly taxing game of croquet. Unwittingly, the implausibly chic Scandinavian beauty has stumbled on to premises owned by her ex-lover, the hard-bitten former gun-runner Rick Blaine (Humphrey Bogart). The pair had met in Paris two years before, but Ilsa unceremoniously left Rick in the lurch, abandoning him to take the last train south alone before the Nazis arrived.

Left, as Rick puts it, 'with a comical look on his face, because his insides have been kicked out', he fled in despair to free French Casablanca. Hoping to escape his painful past, he set up a thriving bar, illicit gambling den and posh knocking-shop which, despite its inauspicious location in the poverty-stricken Maghreb, boasts a full English-speaking big band and a clientele largely consisting of shoulder-padded Hollywood starlets. All in Rick's life seems stable at last, but when Ilsa walks in and asks his piano player Sam (Dooley Wilson) to play their favourite song, 'As Time Goes By', her prettily shod foot kicks the lid off the whole can of worms once again.

She comes with her husband in tow, Czech resistance fighter Victor Laszlo (ironically, played by Austrian aristocrat Paul Henreid), and they are desperate to escape to America before the Nazis nab him definitively. Only Rick has access to the black market letters of transit that would allow them to escape, but he refuses to hand them over. Rick is unable to understand how anyone could prefer a polished, handsome war hero like Laszlo, who is always polite and gracious, to a shady, bibulous old grouch like himself who wears a permanent scowl that gives him the demeanour of an egg-bound duck, albeit a handsome one. But as Ilsa's true motivations for leaving him reveal themselves, Rick (at last!) hatches a plan that shows he is not quite the self-serving misanthrope he appears to be.

While everyone in the film seems dead set on leaving Casablanca as soon as they can, the city's cuisine has its charms, as demonstrated by this rich, subtle sea bass soup.

Casablancan Fish Soup

500g (18 oz) cheap white fish
  (coley, pollack, hoki)
2½ litres (4½ pints) water
2 bay leaves
2 fennel bulbs, trimmed of stalks
100g (4 oz) butter
½ teaspoon grated nutmeg
salt and pepper

4 carrots, peeled
3 sticks celery
3 onions, peeled
¼ teaspoon saffron (optional)
800g (1 lb 12 oz) sea bass, cut
  into 2cm (¾ inch) chunks
1 tablespoon flat-leaf parsley
1 tablespoon coriander

Chop your choice of cheap white fish into small chunks and place in a large saucepan. Cover with the water and add 2 carrots, 2 sticks of celery, 1 onion, chopped, and the bay leaves. Bring to the boil and simmer for 90 minutes. Strain off the ingredients, discard them and set the resulting stock aside. Cut the remaining vegetables and the fennel into small cubes. Melt the butter in a pan and cook the vegetables in it over medium heat for a few minutes. Add the nutmeg and pour the fish stock over. Boil the ingredients gently for 20 minutes. Season the soup with salt and pepper, then add the saffron and sea bass. Simmer for a further 5 to 7 minutes, then serve garnished with a little chopped parsley and coriander.

Serves 4 as a starter.

Gone With the Wind

(Victor Fleming, 1939)

'As God is my witness, I'll never be hungry again!' So cries
Scarlett O'Hara (Vivien Leigh) looking out across the civil-
war-ravaged fields of Tara, her family's once opulent Georgia
estate. It's no wonder the spoilt beauty feels hunger so keenly
– she spent the earlier, happier part of her life trussed up in
frilly dresses that made her look like an enormous cake. Born
rich into a charmed world where the living was easy, where
life was a ball and the slaves would chink their manacles
cheerfully as they toiled in the cotton fields, Scarlett has
taken the South's downfall hard. Now that Union soldiers
have toppled the Confederates, her perplexingly ungrateful
slaves have run off, her father has gone mad and her once
pretty hands look like the side of a box of Swan Vestas.

She soon manages to drag herself out of the muck, however. Dressed sumptuously in a pair of old curtains, she manages to grab her sister's beau for herself and uses his money
to set up a booming timber business. With money flowing in
again and the war's trauma finally fading, Scarlett can now
concentrate on her real dilemma: deciding who the true love
of her life really is. Is it Ashley Wilkes (Leslie Howard), her
noble but married and wimpish neighbour? Or is it smirking,
single Action Man Rhett Butler (Clark Gable), who sees a

kindred spirit in her selfishness and grit? Everyone in the audience can see instantly that Ashley, who looks a bit like Prince Charles crossed with a stick insect, is a whey-faced nonentity. Unfortunately, it takes Scarlett three hours and seventeen minutes to twig that maybe greasily assertive Rhett might be a better bet, despite his wearing a silly pencil moustache that looks like someone drew it on him for a joke. But having toyed with him so long, can she ever make him give a damn again?

This classic Southern recipe harks back to Tara's glory days. It tastes best eaten with your fingers, especially if they have been worn raw from picking Massa's cotton.

Buttermilk Fried Chicken

400ml (14 fl oz) buttermilk (or plain yoghurt)	3 teaspoons paprika
	2 teaspoons cayenne pepper
100ml (4 fl oz) milk	6 large chicken pieces
1 onion, chopped	200g (7½ oz) plain flour
3 tablespoons tarragon and parsley, very finely minced	200ml (7 fl oz) vegetable oil
	lemon wedges

Dilute the buttermilk with the milk, add the onion and half the herbs and spices. Gently beat the chicken flat with a mallet (don't go crazy and rip it) and submerge it in the buttermilk. Coat thoroughly and leave overnight to marinate.

Before cooking, drain the marinade off the chicken in a colander. Put the flour and the remaining herbs and spices in a plastic bag, and shake everything together. Drop the chicken pieces into the bag one by one and shake hard until they are fully coated. Shake any excess coating off lightly. Heat the oil until very hot in a heavy-bottomed frying pan. Put the chicken in the pan and reduce the heat to medium immediately. Fry on both sides – five minutes per side should be enough. Place the chicken on a grill pan (to catch any falling oil), cover with foil and place in a preheated medium oven (190°C/375°F/Mark 5). Bake for 15 minutes to make sure it is cooked through to the bone (this method is not authentically Southern, but it's foolproof).

Serve with mashed potatoes, spring greens and the lemon wedges for squeezing over.

Rebel Without a Cause

(Nicholas Ray, 1955)

What exactly does Jim Stark (James Dean) have to complain about? By modern dramatic standards, his parents seem pretty lenient and well adjusted, he lives in a big house and has a pretty hot car for a teenager – hell, he even looks like James Dean! But despite being dealt a better hand than most, the hunky high school student just can't seem to pull himself out of his funk. Exasperated with his doormat father and bickering mother, Jim is constantly embroiled in fights and scrapes with the cops. His parents try to give him a fresh start in a new town, but things start to go pear-shaped as soon as he arrives. First he is picked up drunk by the cops, then he's snubbed by pouting, bad-girl neighbour Judy (Natalie Wood), despite the fact that she too has had run-ins with the police – for the heinous crime of walking around unchaperoned at night (often the first step into a life of debauchery, I find). Finally, switchblade-wielding greasers at his new school slash his car tires and goad him into playing a game of chicken.

Accompanied by his new friend, lonely oddball Plato (Sal Mineo) – who to modern eyes clearly has a massive and quite understandable crush on Jim – he meets the gang on a nearby clifftop. Jim races Judy's hoodlum boyfriend Buzz (Corey Allen) in a stolen car to the cliff's edge, with a view to seeing who will be cowardly enough to jump out first. When Buzz's car door gets stuck and he ends up splattered on the rocks, everybody makes themselves scarce. You'd think Judy might be a little browned off at seeing her boyfriend speckling the local beauty spot, but she's got Jim now, hasn't she? Running around a deserted house together, the pair even start to enjoy a little simple happiness. But Jim is racked by guilt, and with Buzz's friends out for his blood and a demented (and possibly jealous) Plato running amok with a gun, a big, ugly showdown is clearly just around the corner.

Not only is meatloaf what Jim Stark gets in his lunchtime sandwiches, it's also exactly the sort of classic comfort food that rebellious teens refuse to eat all over America, just to piss their parents off. As ordinary meatloaf is clearly for squares, this recipe bucks the standard formula by adding olives and buckwheat. If you want to make an especially rebellious version of it, eat it with the meat still raw. That'll show the bastards.

Rebel Meatloaf

60g (2 oz) buckwheat
(see p. 264)

2 sticks celery, trimmed of their
strings

1 onion, peeled

30g (1 oz) butter

1 clove garlic, minced

12 pitted green olives, finely
  chopped

300g (10½ oz) lean beef mince

200g (7½ oz) pork mince

1 tablespoon chopped parsley

1 tablespoon chopped chives

1 egg, beaten

50ml (2 fl oz) passata (sieved
  tomatoes)

salt and black pepper to taste

1 teaspoon lemon juice (optional)

Plus

1 loaf tin

greaseproof paper

For the sauce

1 onion, chopped

20g (¾ oz) butter

2 cloves garlic, chopped

150ml (5 fl oz) passata

50ml (2 fl oz) water

¼ teaspoon ground nutmeg

Boil the buckwheat in water for 15 minutes, then drain it fully and leave it to cool. Chop the celery and onion into very small dice. Melt the butter in a pan and cook these vegetables gently in it until soft and translucent (5–8 minutes). Add the garlic and olives and cook for 2 further minutes. Crumble the cooled buckwheat into fine rubble by rubbing it between your hands or whizzing it in a blender, then knead this into the meat. Add the herbs, egg, passata, salt and pepper and lemon juice plus the cooked olive/onion/celery and mix well – it's important to do this thoroughly, or the loaf may be prone to crumbling when cooked.

Turn the mixture into a loaf tin lined with greaseproof paper, coaxing it into a smooth loaf shape. Bake in the middle of an oven preheated to 190°C/375°F/Mark 5 for one hour. Halfway through the cooking, take the loaf out of the oven, pour off any liquid it has shed, and return to the oven. When it is done, leave it to cool slightly, then carefully lift it out on the paper and transfer to a dish.

To make the sauce, soften the onion in the butter until translucent in a frying pan, then add the garlic and cook a minute longer. Add the passata, water and nutmeg and bring to the boil. Simmer down to a thick, barely runny sauce and pour it over the loaf.

Serve sliced with mashed potatoes or rice.

Some Like It Hot

(Billy Wilder, 1959)

In a world full of dodgy female impersonators, Tony Curtis and Jack Lemmon might just be the worst. Trying desperately to hold their Cupid's bow pouts while tottering hopelessly at over six feet in their heels, they look like a pair of hod carriers ordered at gunpoint to imitate the late Queen Mother. Mind you, that isn't all that far from the truth of the matter. As down-at-heel Chicago jazz players Joe and Jerry, they find donning women's clothes is the only safe way to get out of town when they become accidental witnesses to the St Valentine's Day Massacre. With Chicago crawling with goons hungry for their blood, they grab the first effective chance of escape they can find, disguising themselves ineptly as 'Josephine' and 'Daphne' and joining a women-only jazz troupe bound for Florida.

Hobbling on to the train heading south and to safety, they pal up with Sugar Kane Kowalczyk (Marilyn Monroe), a wildly curvaceous singer with their new band whose wiggle makes her backside look 'like jello on springs', as Jerry puts it. They find her so arousing that when she crawls into Jerry's sleeper for a nightcap, instead of maidenly blushing at her skimpy nightgown, he finds his blood rushing elsewhere. Joe, meanwhile, is so besotted with Sugar that when they reach

Florida he imitates a bachelor millionaire (in a broad caricature of Cary Grant) in order to woo her, with great success.
This leaves Jerry stuck fending off a genuine millionaire in
the shape of Osgood Fielding III (Joe E. Brown), a horny old
ram given to grabbing at Daphne's behind while they rumba.
However, when the gangster they're on the run from turns
up at the hotel, their worries switch from keeping randy men
out of their beds to wondering whether they'll wake up one
morning cheek to cheek with a severed horse's head.

These suggestively shaped desserts get their name from their
resemblance to the glands which Sugar possesses in such
plump abundance, but which Joe and Jerry are so sorely
lacking. In other words, they look like a pair of tits.

Frozen Raspberry Tits

250g (9 oz) raspberries	4 eggs
3 level teaspoons caster sugar	150g (5½ oz) icing sugar
juice of half a lemon	300ml (10 fl oz) double cream
125g (4½ oz) meringues	

Press the raspberries through a sieve, holding 2 back, until only
the pips remain behind. Add the caster sugar and the lemon juice

to the sieved pulp. Put the meringues in a plastic bag and crush gently but thoroughly with a rolling pin. Whisk the eggs very thoroughly in a bowl, then very slowly add first the icing sugar, then the meringue, whisking as you go. In a separate bowl whisk the cream until firm, then fold it carefully into the egg mixture. When they are fully amalgamated add the raspberry pulp and fold in carefully as before.

Scoop the mixture into two bowl-shaped moulds of roughly a litre each. If you don't have these, the basins that Christmas puddings come in make an excellent substitute. Smooth the mixture flat, then cover each bowl with cling film that you have moistened slightly. Place in the freezer for at least 12 hours.

To serve, dip the bowls in warm water to loosen the desserts, then turn out on to a plate. For ideal results, return them to the freezer for another half-hour. Before serving, use the last two raspberries to make a 'nipple' in the centre of each pudding.

Breakfast at Tiffany's

(Blake Edwards, 1961)

Eating a roll while staring through a shop window might not be everyone's idea of a pick-me-up, but it seems to work for Holly Golightly. The giddy, exquisitely beautiful socialite (Audrey Hepburn) lives a boozy, precarious life getting by on her wits alone on the rough edges of New York's smart set. She lives a social whirl where she never sleeps before dawn, and parties in her bare apartment are thronged with well-connected drunkards and imposing society women, many of whom appear to be wearing small, elaborate lampshades on their heads.

Holly just about manages to eke out her glamorous existence by cajoling 'money for the powder room' out of wealthy dinner companions. Unfortunately, most expect something in return and she spends her evenings fending off randy and inebriated suitors, or her cartoonish neighbour Mr Yunioshi (a dire Japanese caricature by Mickey Rooney). When things get too much for her, as they often do, she cheers herself up by taking her breakfast down to jewellery store Tiffany's, whose air of dependable luxury always makes her feel better.

Holly thinks her luck has turned for the better, however, when she meets a prim but dashing Brazilian millionaire (José da Silva Pereira) who looks like he might be husband material. Trouble is, she's already smitten with Paul Varjak (George Peppard, better known as Hannibal from *The A-Team*), the gigolo and frustrated writer upstairs, the one person who doesn't try to take advantage of her. But she can't decide between the two. Should she choose a dependable but dull existence as elegant arm candy for her South American, with only the occasional military coup to divert her during days spent knitting ponchos for her Brazilian brood? Or should she plump for (only marginally less insipid) Paul, and an exciting, unreliable life on the run with B.A, Baracas, righting wrongs with a cannon made out of a hairdryer?

As Holly seems to drink far more than she eats, the breakfast at Tiffany's below is of the liquid variety. This cocktail is a version of the classic Dutch Breakfast, using nutty Frangelico (see p. 268) instead of the usual (more herbal) Galliano.

Dutch Breakfast at Tiffany's

ice
200ml (7 fl oz) gin
200ml (7 fl oz) advocaat
50ml (2 fl oz) sugar syrup
2 teaspoons orange zest, in fine
   strands

25ml (1 tablespoon) Frangelico
50ml (2 fl oz) lime juice
50ml (2 fl oz) lemon juice

Fill a cocktail shaker and two large tumblers with ice. Pour the alcohol, fruit juices and syrup (see *Arctic Martini Granita*, p. 66, for how to make this) into the shaker and shake thoroughly until condensation forms on the outside. Strain into the chilled glasses, add the orange zest, and serve. If you prefer a longer drink, this cocktail also works well diluted with soda water.

Swept Away

(Guy Ritchie, 2002)

Women, eh? They throw their weight around and try to drag men down to their level – but all they really want is to be slapped about, starved and forced to rub octopuses on rocks. Well, that seems to be the gist of Guy Ritchie's film. In its opening scenes, we meet venomous, charm-free heiress Amber Leighton (Madonna), arriving in Greece to begin a yacht cruise with her weakling husband and dull friends. A diehard material girl, she's so glossily opulent she looks as if she's been dipped in gold dust like a lollipop in sherbet, and finds little to amuse her on board the unluxurious ship. In fact, the only pastime that gives her any satisfaction is goading smouldering Communist deckhand Giuseppe (Adriano Giannini), who seems to have been cast as an Italian solely so he can get away with speaking just-one-Cornetto English instead of subtitled Greek with the other crew members.

Amber winds Giuseppe up by alternately shaking her shiny bits at him and snubbing him with witless, leaden putdowns. But this shrew is due to be tamed. When a motorboat they are in breaks down, Amber and Giuseppe find themselves washed up alone on the sort of cinematic uninhabited island that can be seen from miles away but is mysteriously invisible to the yacht crew searching for them. Deprived of creature comforts, flattering lighting or a decent script, cracks start to appear in Amber's haughty mask as she is forced to rely on Giuseppe to survive. He in turn decides to pay her back in kind for her previous bitchery, making her wash his clothes, clean his fish and call him master in return for food.

Reduced to bedraggled fishwife, suck slave and slap target, Amber does the natural womanly thing and falls deeply in love with Giuseppe, who inexplicably concludes that there must be a heart beating somewhere under her wooden exterior. They spend a few blissful days together, drinking some meths they find in an old shed, playing charades and rolling around sexlessly on the sand, chastely clad in swimsuits (despite being observed by nothing but the odd grasshopper). But notwithstanding Giuseppe's miraculous ability to find fresh water and bountiful provisions on a bare rock, their idyll has to end. The couple's unlikely love for each other, and the audience's patience, can only last so long before the film disappears, *Titanic*-style, under the sea of its own failed ambitions.

Char-grilled Baby Octopus

30 baby octopuses (fresh or, more realistically, frozen and defrosted; see p. 268), ink sacks removed
250ml (8 fl oz) vegetable stock
1 glass dry white wine
2 leeks
2 sticks celery

2 bay leaves
1 teaspoon oregano
½ teaspoon chilli flakes
1 tablespoon balsamic vinegar
4 cloves garlic, chopped
2 teaspoons ground black pepper

Plus

skewers

Soak the octopuses in water for an hour, changing the water twice (this helps remove any grit in them). Put the stock and wine into a pan and bring to the boil. Add the octopuses, leeks and celery and simmer for 30–40 minutes, until the octopuses are tender. Leave the pot to cool, then stir in the remaining ingredients and leave overnight in the fridge.

Drain the octopuses, thread them on skewers and grill over charcoal until crispy. The liquid they were stewed in plays no other part in the dish, but can be strained and used as a stock for a fish or vegetable soup.

Serve the octopus with a salad of lettuce hearts and flat-leaf parsley.

Showgirls

(Paul Verhoeven, 1995)

Dancer Nomi Malone (Elizabeth Berkley) is a drab-featured nonentity with the allure of a punnet of sausage meat and the brainpower of a newt. As she is determined to claw her way to the top of Las Vegas's gruesome entertainment world, you might think this would pose a problem. And sure enough, when she first hitch-hikes into town with nothing but a flick-knife and the proverbial suitcase full of dreams (though the suitcase itself is quickly stolen), the only place she can find to ply her dubious talents is Cheetah's, a sleazy club where she works as a pole-humping stripper.

Her burning ambition, however, is to dance in the show at the Sunset Casino, a gloriously trashy spectacle involving what look like Butlin's redcoats hoofing around half-starkers wrapped in tinfoil, with more pert nipples than a dairy farm of lactating cows. Despite her charmless vacuity (she's not called 'No Me' for nothing), we are expected to applaud Nomi's scrabble for fame, and not find it odd when everyone around her wants to help her for no reward.

Nomi finally gets her chance when the Sunset's big star, trout-pouted Cristal Connors (Gina Gershon), drops into Cheetah's with her embarrassed lover Zack Carey (Kyle MacLachlan), the casino's entertainment manager. Nomi is humiliated when Cristal forces her to lap-dance Zack while she watches. But Cristal finds her prime lap-dance move – a sort of wobbly whiplash grind that recalls an elephant seal fleeing a hungry polar bear – so enticing that she gets her an audition for the Sunset's chorus line.

Nomi gets the role, but the glitter of the chorus line turns out to be tarnished. For starters, Nomi sees one dancer trip up another, who crashes down on her knee (upon which a physiotherapist rushes on stage and grabs it hard and waggles it – she winces – 'It's her knee,' he explains). Then she finds herself sparring with Cristal in a spot of amateur-dramatic lesbo vamping (sample lines: 'I like nice tits – how about you?' 'I like having nice tits'). Grimly fixated on supplanting Cristal, Nomi will let nothing get in her way. But despite her increasing ruthlessness, will her ambition waver as she finally starts to notice that the backbiting and neon-lit swimming pools around her might just be a teensy-weensy bit tawdry?

In one of many bizarre scenes, Nomi and Cristal both confess to loving dog food when they were children (a heavy-handed way of pointing out that they are supposed to be complete bitches?). This dish – a canine version of *Tournedos Rossini* with added bone marrow (it makes their coats glossier, apparently) – is a luxury offering for pampered pooches on the up, and a perfect accompaniment for a film which is, after all, an utter dog's dinner already.

Gourmet Doggie Chow

4 beef marrow bones	olive oil
4 fillet steaks, roughly 150g	250g (9 oz) foie gras
(5½ oz) each	100ml (4 fl oz) Madeira
butter	½ truffle (optional), finely chopped

Put the marrow bones in an oven dish and bake them in a medium oven for 1 hour. Using a skewer, scrape out the now jelly-like marrow from inside the bones and set it aside. Brown the steaks on both sides in some butter and the olive oil in a hot pan, ensuring that they remain reasonably rare in the centre. I usually cook mine for 2 minutes a side, but you must go by your own tastes (though cooking them entirely through would be a waste of good meat!). Set these aside on a covered plate.

Cut the foie gras into 4 slices and brown each briefly in more (foaming) butter. Set aside and cover. Pour the Madeira into the pan, add the marrow and truffle and scrape the bottom with a wooden spoon to dislodge any meat juices. Bubble down briefly to a thick sauce.

Slice the steaks into bite-sized chunks and place in four dog bowls. Top each chunk with a little piece of foie gras and pour over the Madeira sauce. Dogs will prefer this when it is properly cooled, but humans should eat immediately, with no hands.

Catwoman

(Pitof, 2004)

Patience Phillips (Halle Berry) is a woman wronged. Working as a lowly, Ally McBealish (gawky, professionally inept) graphic artist in a massive cosmetics company, she is a dowdy underpaid mouse (we are asked to believe), despite having looks that could melt the icecaps and a flat like a millionaire banker's city shag pad.

But this all changes when one night, while, for some reason, she is stalking around her employer's factory, she accidentally overhears some startling revelations about its new anti-ageing cream's devastating long-term effects. Company goons discover her, and silence her by flushing her out of the drains into a nearby river, where she drowns. Thankfully, one of those 4,000-year-old life-giving cats is on the island where she washes up, and its enchanted halitosis is so pungent that it brings her back to life when it tries to French-kiss her. Reincarnated as an ass-kicking, leather-clad semi-feline, she starts gobbling sushi, rolling her Rs and, erm, excelling at basketball – just like a real cat, then.

No longer the faux-wallflower, she develops a foolproof scheme to bring her murderers to justice and expose the new beauty cream's evil effects. Keeping a necessarily low profile by prancing around town in adolescent wank-fantasy bondage gear (whip included), she battles the baddies by habitually dropping in to warn them that she's got their number. But surrounded by acting that would shame a panto and by a flurry of cheap video-game CGI, Catwoman is quite naturally full of doubts. Will she always affect aching sincerity, despite a backdrop of what looks like a series of bad R 'n' B video outtakes? Or will she finally wake up and realize that she's playing a PVC pussy in a bit of camp silliness, rather than Cleopatra on her deathbed?

The audience also is left in temporarily agonizing confusion. When it comes to the evil cream designed to manipulate women's insecurity, who is the real enemy? The male-dominated company, perchance? Or is it actually the boss's wife and past-it former model Laurel Hedare (Sharon Stone), taking out her bitterness at ageing by mutilating the rest of womankind? Have a guess. Fortunately womankind has lithe, hard-bodied young Catwoman to lash the trumped-up old trout back into her place at the bottom of the pecking order, striking a victory for feminism, empowerment and push-up bras. Or something like that.

With her voracious appetite for cream, Catwoman would surely approve of this extremely simple but delicious dessert. If you want to make it even more of a feline treat, serve it in a saucer garnished with thin slivers of tuna sashimi.

THE RAZZIES

Cream Posset

zest of 1 lemon (ideally,
    unwaxed)
100g (4 oz) caster sugar

500ml (17 fl oz) double cream
5 tablespoons fortified sweet
    wine (Madeira, port, sherry)

Strip any white pith off the lemon zest and slice into the finest strands you can manage. Place in a bowl and cover with boiling water. Leave for a few minutes, then strain. Place the sugar and cream in a saucepan and bring gently to the boil. Simmer for 2–3 minutes, then leave to cool until you can bear to stick a finger in it for more than a second. Stir in the fortified wine and the lemon zest and blend thoroughly. Spoon the posset into glasses and leave to set in the fridge for at least 3 hours.

If you don't go for the tuna garnish, serve this dessert with shortbread fingers.

Filmes de langue étrangère

Pelliculas de lengua extranjera

外国語映画

Fremdsprachige Filme

I film in lingua straniera

Buitenlandse taal films

Filmes de lingua estrangeira

фильмы иностранного языка

Utländska filmer

Foreign language films

Good Bye, Lenin!

(Wolfgang Becker, 2003)

Who says that life in the old Eastern Bloc was so bad? Sure, there was the constant presence of the secret police, the persecution of political dissidents, severe restrictions on travel, the stifling of genuine public debate, appalling environmental pollution, a lack of genuine opportunities or proper contraception and a chronic shortage of bathplugs, non-polyester clothing and soft toilet paper. But that's only half the story: they also had cute children's cartoons, nice songs about Lenin and cars that looked like toys for toddlers (but unfortunately weren't).

With all that to lose, it's not so surprising that East Berlin resident and Communist activist Christiane Kerner (Katrin Sass) is a little nervous about the shaky political situation in the German Democratic Republic. It's 1989, and while people are fleeing the country by any means possible, Christiane has been invited to a dinner for Party bigwigs to celebrate the republic's fortieth birthday. On her way to the bash, she sees her son Alex (Daniel Bruhl) being arrested by riot police and suffers a massive heart attack from the shock. Falling into a coma, she lies unconscious for eight months. When she awakens, the Berlin Wall has fallen, her daughter's got a new job dishing up instant botulism at Burger King and the socialist system she worked so hard for has gone the way of the dodo.

Fearing her heart is too weak to bear the shock, Alex pretends to his bed-bound mother that nothing has changed, and that all the old guard are still in place. He recreates the old conditions in their little flat, bringing back the flimsy chipboard furniture from the cellar and clothing himself and his sister in the Communist Crimplene horrors that everybody else has just binned. In mimicking the bad old days, food proves the hardest part. Alex finds himself rummaging through abandoned flats and refilling old jars to feed his mother's cravings for the pickled stodge considered a luxury before the fall. But with Coca-Cola ads being unfurled in place of propaganda posters and Christiane slowly regaining the ability to walk, it's only a matter of time before she realizes that the socialist workers' and farmers' state she lives in is as real as the Tooth Fairy.

This Russian soup was long a favourite in the old East Germany, partly because it doesn't require many fresh ingredients but still tastes good. Still a popular choice in many restaurants, it has proved more durable than steroidally enhanced female shot-putters, cars made of reinforced plastic and the art of informing on your neighbours.

Solyanka Soup

1 tablespoon dried porcini
   mushrooms (optional)
4 carrots
2 leeks
4 sticks celery
1.5 litres (2½ pints) boiling
   water
some beef or chicken bones
   (ideally a roast-chicken
   carcase)
2 onions
2 cloves garlic
oil
2 gherkins, chopped

100g (4 oz) sauerkraut
8 juniper berries
1 tablespoon tomato purée
1 bay leaf
100g (4 oz) small closed-cup
   mushrooms, quartered
150g (5½ oz) smoked pork loin
   (see p. 269)
1 dried Polish kabanos sausage
   (optional, see p. 266)
2 heaped tablespoons chopped
   dill
4 heaped teaspoons sour cream
   or crème fraiche

If you are using them, put the porcini in a bowl, cover them with a little boiling water and leave to soak. Cut the carrots, leeks and celery into chunks and put in a large saucepan. Cover with the water, add the bones and bring to the boil. Simmer covered for 1 hour, then discard the bones and vegetables, squeezing the latter briefly in a sieve to extract the last juices.

Peel and chop the onions and garlic and put in a large pan (it can be the same one used to make the stock) with a little oil. Cook until soft and translucent. Add the gherkins and sauerkraut, then pour in the broth. Add the juniper berries, tomato purée and bay leaf and bring to the boil. Chop the porcini finely, and add to the pot, along with their soaking liquid and the closed-cup mushrooms. Cover on a low simmer and cook for 30 minutes.

Chop the pork loin and sausage into small chunks and add to the pot. Cook for another 15 minutes. Remove from the heat and stir in the dill.

Serve in four bowls with a spoonful of sour cream and a little extra chopped dill on top.

Amélie

(Jean-Pierre Jeunet, 2001)

Pretty young café waitress and Snow White look-alike Amélie
Poulain (Audrey Tautou) lives in Paris – not the real one,
of course, full of traffic, tourists and even (whisper it) the
occasional immigrant. No, she lives in an exquisitely white-
washed fantasy Paris full of lovable artistic invalids, failed
writers, former circus performers and shop assistants with
charming learning difficulties. It's a dreamy place where a waitress can afford to live in a gorgeous flat in pricey Montmartre,
and still have plenty of time to collect skimming stones, bake
cakes and take an afternoon off whenever the plot demands;
a place where no piece of music sounds less than thirty years
old, where the clouds are teddy-bear-shaped and the only real
danger is being drowned in a tidal wave of syrup.

Despite the glittering surface of her world, though, things
haven't always been smooth for Amélie – she's a complete
misfit, apparently (you know, one of those cinematic misfits
with model good looks, a decent job and lots of friends). The
child of obsessive strait-laced parents, she is brought up by
her distant father alone after a suicidal Québécois tourist
jumps off a church and on to her mother. Retreating into
a world of make-believe from which she never emerges, she
whiles her life away daydreaming, imagining how many

couples in Paris are having orgasms (fifteen!), or listening to spoons cracking the sugar crust on a crème brûlée. But when she discovers a child's box of treasures from the 50s hidden behind a tile in her bathroom, she decides to get out into the real(ish) world and restore it to its original owner.

He's so delighted to get it back that Amélie now devotes herself to full-time do-gooding. Whether she's setting up customers at her café or consoling her heartbroken concierge, she sprinkles a Milky Way of winsome fairy dust wherever she pokes her dainty nose.

But while she perks up those around her, what of little Amélie's chances of love? Things look like they might improve when she spots another pretty, ineffectual geek, Nino Quincampoix (Mathieu Kassovitz – who, ironically enough, directed the ultra-gritty, violent ghetto drama *La Haine*). As Nino drives a girly scooter, was bullied at school and spends his days working in a dildo shop, an astute observer might deduce that he isn't necessarily the marrying kind. But as he has his own whimsical obsession – collecting discarded photo-booth snaps – Amélie fixates on him and seeks to lure him to a rendezvous. But will she have the courage to talk to him, or will she spend her life forever living in a cutesy dream world that makes *The House at Pooh Corner* look like *The 120 Days of Sodom*?

As it's a quaint, nostalgic French movie, *Amélie* is absolutely bursting with food, out of which I've chosen this recipe, one of the daily dishes served up in her café. Like the Paris of the film, it's extremely old-fashioned and pure-bloodedly French – but a little goes a long way.

FOREIGN LANGUAGE FILMS

Chicory and Ham Gratin

100ml (4 fl oz) water
140g (5 oz) butter
8 heads chicory
2 cloves garlic, finely minced
3 tablespoons plain flour
200–250ml (7–8 fl oz) milk

salt and pepper
¼ teaspoon nutmeg
8 large slices cooked ham,
   any fat removed
300g (10½ oz) Gruyère, grated

Heat the water and 40g (1½ oz) of the butter in a large casserole, add the chicory and cover. Bring to a low simmer; then after 10 minutes, add the garlic. Cook on the lowest heat possible for another half-hour, turning several times, until the chicory is tender all the way through – prod them with a knife to check that the chicory hearts have softened. Reserving their cooking liquid, leave them to drain in a colander for at least 30 minutes, as they have a tendency to hold a lot of liquid which can spoil the sauce later.

When they are almost drained, make the sauce. Melt the remaining butter in a saucepan. Remove from the heat and stir in the flour to create a thin paste. Add any remaining cooking liquid from the chicory and beat into the paste. Return to the heat and add the milk a little at a time, stirring constantly to make a thick creamy sauce. Bring the sauce to a low boil and cook for 1 further minute. 200ml (7 fl oz) of milk should be enough to create a thick sauce that is still fluid after the boiling, but add up to another 50ml (2 fl oz) if it looks in danger of drying out before it is cooked through. Remove from the heat, and season with the salt, pepper and nutmeg.

Squeeze each head of chicory gently to remove any remaining liquid, then wrap them in the slices of ham. Place them in a buttered oven dish and sprinkle over the gruyère. Pour the sauce on top and bake in an oven preheated to 200°C/400°F/Mark 6 for 20 minutes.

As the gratin is very rich, it's perhaps best served just with bread, with a green salad to follow.

In the Mood for Love

(Wong Kar-wai, 2000)

Being cheated on is never a bundle of laughs, but knowing your husband is having it away surreptitiously behind a few inches of masonry in the room next door must be especially galling. This is the grim situation that Hong Kong secretary Su Li-zhen (Maggie Cheung) finds herself in. It's the early 1960s and, as there's scarcely room to swing a gerbil in the crowded colony and flats are scarce, she and her husband (whose face we never see) rent a single room in a shared flat. As she has to run the gauntlet of chattering mah-jong players in the kitchen whenever she fancies so much as a cup of tea, Su Li-zhen and her husband get very little privacy. As if this weren't enough, her husband's work suddenly takes him away from home more than ever before – so what's going on?

The answer is just feet away in the room rented by dapper shipping clerk Chow Mo-wan (Tony Leung Chiu-wai) and his wife. With both of their partners permanently tied up with 'business', Chow Mo-wan and Su Li-zhen soon come to the painful conclusion that their spouses are having a fling. But how could it have happened? Each of the spurned spouses has matinée idol good looks. Could it be that the money Su Li-zhen spent on the implausibly numerous (twenty-five) and utterly stylish cheongsams she sports in the film led her husband in despair to find a cheaper date? Or was the constant hum of Nat King Cole that seems to follow Chow Mo-wan wherever he goes starting to grate on his wife's nerves?

Reeling from the shock of betrayal and afraid to confront them, the couple try to piece together the process leading to their partners' infidelity. They go out for dinner, walk arm in arm, trying to imagine who said what and who made the first move. But although they are armed with a sense of moral superiority over their love-rat spouses, the couple's lonely evenings slowly turn into something bittersweet: could they, like their wayward spouses, be about to take the primrose path of dalliance too?

Li-zhen and Mo-wan first take proper notice of each other when they cross on their sad, solitary way to the local noodle stall, and it is when we see each of them dining solo that their isolation is clearest.

When it comes to eating a Chinese dumpling with an air of suppressed melancholy, Tony Leung is a world master. I enjoy these wonton steamed, but they also work well boiled and served up in clear chicken broth.

Prawn and Mushroom Wonton

8 dried Chinese mushrooms
   (shiitake will do fine, although
   not strictly Chinese)
200g (7½ oz) shelled prawns
200g (7½ oz) tofu (ideally, firm
   rather than silky)
2 teaspoons sesame oil
2 teaspoons soy sauce

2 tablespoons peanut oil
2 cloves garlic, finely chopped
1½ teaspoons grated fresh
   ginger
2 heaped tablespoons chopped
   chives
1 pack round wonton wrappers
   (about 50; see p. 270)

For the dipping sauce

6 tablespoons soy sauce
3 tablespoons sesame oil
3 tablespoons rice wine vinegar

1 teaspoon sesame seeds
   (optional)

Put the mushrooms in a bowl and cover with boiling water. Leave to soak until soft and malleable (at least half an hour). Squeeze dry and chop as fine as you can. Chop the prawns into small chunks, and break the tofu into a crumbly mass. Place in a bowl with the sesame oil and soy sauce and leave to stand. Heat the peanut oil in a wok and fry the garlic, ginger, mushrooms and chives for around 30 seconds, removing them as soon as the garlic starts to take colour. Stir into the prawn and tofu mixture and mix fully.

Take the wrappers one at a time. Place a small teaspoonful of the stuffing in the centre of the wrapper. Moisten your finger with water and dampen one edge of the wrapper, then fold the other edge over and press tightly closed. Seal the newly bonded edge even more firmly by pinching it into a frill. Set aside and repeat until all the wrappers are filled. Place the wonton in a steamer over boiling water and steam for 10 minutes.

Mix the ingredients for the dipping sauce and serve.

Together

(Lukas Moodysson, 2000)

No TV, no meat, no Coca-Cola, no Christmas presents, atrocious hippy music blaring constantly and little boys in girls' plimsolls named after offensives in the Vietnam war – young Eva (Emma Samuelsson) and Stefan (Sam Kessel) are quite understandably disgusted when their mother Elisabeth (Lisa Lindgren) moves them into this haven of discord, her brother's hippy commune in Stockholm.

Still, with their alcoholic father slapping their mother around back home, the children have little choice but to move out. Packing their belongings into the commune's utterly rubbish camper van, they soon find their chaotic new home isn't that much more peaceful than the old one. Among the residents are a posh Marxist radical who prefers ranting on about the profit motive to having sex, a puritanical couple who'd rather move out than let their kid watch telly, a gay doormat who tries to wheedle blow jobs out of a straight man whenever he's not stuck behind his loom, and a newly lesbian mother given to going bottomless so as to air her fungal infection. Match them with a spoilt cow who lovingly details her sexual escapades to her long-suffering boyfriend, and you have a perfect recipe for constant bickering.

All the same, while Eva and Stefan hate the food, the

people, the music and the clothes, it's not all misery. Stefan spends some happy times with the other politically aware seven-year-old in the commune, pretending to be fascist South American torture squads, or playing with the two pieces of wooden 'Lego' that one of the dads has whittled for them. Eva, meanwhile, makes friends with the equally geeky boy next door, despite his uptight parents' not entirely unjustified conviction that the commune is a nest of twisted anarchist sex vixens.

Exposed to radicalism at an early age, the children start a campaign of their own: for the right to watch television and eat meat. With Eva and Stefan's drunk dad Rolf (Mikael Nyqvist) sobering up and realizing he's just flushed his family down the toilet, and the most self-righteous of the communards fleeing the oncoming introduction of meat and Mickey Mouse, commune life is slowly starting to look bearable. Almost.

When the kids successfully put meat back on the menu, the remaining self-denying hippies junk their scruples and gleefully tuck in. This unusually flavoured pork dish is a version of a traditional Swedish favourite for special occasions, and is considerably richer in taste than the grim mess of lumpy porridge that typifies the commune.

Pork Loin with Prunes and Caraway

150ml (5 fl oz) stock
8 prunes
800g (1 lb 12 oz) pork loin
2 teaspoons caraway seeds
1 teaspoon mustard
salt and pepper
250g (9 oz) thin slices of
   pancetta, or streaky bacon

6 shallots
1 bay leaf
2 cloves
100ml (4 fl oz) single cream
   (optional – add extra stock
   if not using)

Plus

string

Warm the stock and pour over the prunes. Leave to soak over-night, then squeeze gently dry and reserve the liquid as well as the fruit. Using a sharp knife, cut a lengthwise slit in the pork loin, so that it can be opened up for stuffing. Rub the caraway seeds, mustard, salt and pepper into the cavity, then line it with the prunes. Fold the loin shut, then wrap it in the pancetta or bacon. Tie the meat securely with string and place in a greased oven dish. Chop the shallots and place around the meat. Add the bay leaf and cloves to the shallots and place the dish in the middle of an oven preheated to 180°C/350°F/Mark 4. Bake for 30 minutes, then remove the meat and leave covered somewhere warm. Heat the dish on the hob and add the reserved stock and the cream.

Boil until thick, scraping the pan with a spoon to dislodge any juices. Remove the cloves and bay leaf and pour the sauce over the loin.

Serve sliced, with mashed potatoes and buttered peas.

Women on the Verge
of a Nervous Breakdown

(Pedro Almodóvar, 1988)

If you can't keep your man by means of your charm, you can always drug him. Or so thinks cracked actress Pepa (Carmen Maura) when her no-good lover Iván (Fernando Guillén) tries to sneak out the backdoor of their relationship. Pepa is famous for playing the mother of a serial killer on a trash TV show, but when her man dumps her for another woman, her life starts unravelling in ways that make your average daytime soap seem like the shipping forecast.

First there's the soup: desperate to keep Iván, Pepa laces his favourite gazpacho with sleeping pills and leaves it in her fridge, hoping to knock him flat when he comes back for his belongings. He never returns, but she does manage to sedate Iván's awful daughter-in-law-to-be, a telephone repairman and some police detectives who all turn up at Pepa's penthouse, so her plans aren't a total wash-out.

But why are the police there anyway? They're after the Shiite terrorists, of course – the ones who have used Pepa's ditsy friend Candela's (María Barranco) flat as a weapons depot in return for sex. When, after a weekend fling, Candela is left with nothing but love bites and a flat full of kalashnikovs to remind her of the good times, she realizes her recent squeeze must have been one of the wanted fugitives on the

TV news. She runs round to Pepa's flat seeking help, but finds her friend is too wrapped up in an unexpected visit from Iván's long-lost son Carlos (Antonio Banderas) to really give a toss.

As if the Shiites and the drugged soup weren't enough, Iván's demented ex-wife Lucia (Julieta Serrano) is out for Pepa's blood as well. Swanning around Madrid dressed like an early 60s Doris Day despite a face so heavy with make-up it could make a horse rear in terror, Lucia looks like she's wandered by accident off the set of *Whatever Happened to Baby Jane?*.

By now the audience is starting to wonder, Is there a single woman left in Madrid who hasn't slept with Iván? And isn't he just a little old for all his girlfriends, or are silver foxes considered especially hot in Spain? Either way, his ex-wife is determined to get her own back on the man who sent her loopy in the first place, and to look as camp as she possibly can while doing so. With Lucia coming over to have things out with the strumpet she thinks stole her man, can Pepa stop changing her clothes for one minute and sort out the soupy terroristic drug mess she and all her friends are wallowing in?

Gazpacho

1 kg (2¼lb) properly ripe tomatoes (deep red, and slightly giving to the squeeze)

1 cucumber

1 green pepper

1 small or half a medium onion, peeled

2 cloves garlic, peeled

2 tablespoons good olive oil

1 tablespoon wine vinegar

2 slices decent white bread, crusts removed

salt and pepper

ice cubes

1 stick celery, strings removed and chopped into miniature dice (optional)

1 tablespoon flat-leaf parsley, finely chopped, to garnish (also optional)

Score a little cross in the skin of each tomato. Cover them with boiling water and leave them for 30 seconds, then drain. Peel off the skins and quarter the tomatoes. Chop the cucumber and green pepper into little chunks. Mince the onion and garlic finely. Put the vegetables, the oil and the vinegar in a blender and blend to a fine liquid. Cut the bread into little chunks and add one by one to the blender, pulsing until it is completely amalgamated. If your tomatoes are not heavily ripe, you may need to add a little water here to keep the soap properly liquid.

Pour into a bowl and season (I occasionally add a few drops of extra vinegar here to make it more refreshing, but go by your own tastes). Leave in the fridge to chill fully for two hours, then serve with a few ice cubes floating on top.

Serve in glasses or in bowls, with a little chopped celery and/or parsley sprinkled on top, if you like.

historical
Epics

Gladiator

(Ridley Scott, 2000)

Why won't Maximus Decimus Meridius (Russell Crowe) die? During *Gladiator* he evades an entire Roman legion, fights off what looks like a bunch of unwashed German roadies, laughs in the face of a pair of gay giraffes, slaughters a horde of Amazons in chariots, slices a troupe of tigers into Kit-e-Kat, and vanquishes an army of Martian mutants who have wandered in from another film. OK, so I lied about the giraffes, but you get the idea.

After the death of his great protector Emperor Marcus Aurelius (Richard Harris), the invincible veteran general gets on the wrong side of the old man's quiveringly loopy son Commodus (Joaquin Phoenix). As befits a man named after a portable toilet, Commodus is a dirty trickster with the fishy eyes and barely suppressed yearning to jump his sister that we've come to expect from any Roman emperor worth his perverted salt. Mad as a brush, he was nonetheless mortified to learn that the dying emperor favoured Maximus over him as heir to the Empire, and so strangled his poor dad. Maximus is due for the chop too – but Commodus hasn't counted on his almost supernatural ability to cheat death. True to form, Maximus slays the men sent to kill him and gallops from Germany home to Spain, only to find that his wife and son have been murdered.

But Maximus's travelling days are far from over. Captured and sold into slavery, his next port of call is North Africa, where he is hawked to weary showman Proximo (Oliver Reed) to fight as a gladiator. Not many men survive the arena, but given his general invincibility, Maximus shakes off sword blows much in the manner Audrey Hepburn might shrug off a mink stole. His success gets him plucked from the ranks of javelin fodder and kicked upstairs into the first division, to fight in Rome's Colosseum. Maximus is awed by Ridley Scott's splendidly over-the-top, quasi-fascist CGI fantasy of Rome, and Rome returns the compliment, idolizing his feats in the arena even once his true identity – hitherto concealed – has been revealed.

Commodus knows his old nemesis is returning to haunt him, but is afraid to make a martyr of Maximus by killing him openly. As a final showdown approaches, can Maximus be sure that his soup won't be poisoned before he gets a face-off with the imperial loon himself?

Barley formed the staple of gladiators' diets, and is a major component of this stewy soup using ingredients popular in Classical Rome. The stew would have been seasoned with *garum* (a sauce made by fermenting fish in brine), the ketchup of the Roman Empire. South-East Asians make a very similar condiment, called *nuoc mam* in Vietnam and *nam pla* in Thailand, which makes a good substitute and is far more pleasant and mild-tasting than it sounds. If you can't get hold of this, try using soy sauce with an anchovy in it (which will taste rather fishier).

Ancient Roman Barley Stew

6 carrots

6 sticks celery

4 medium onions

½ head green cabbage

1 chicken carcase

1½ litres (2½ pints) water

2 bay leaves

1 tablespoon flat-leaf parsley, finely chopped

1 tablespoon dried porcini mushrooms

4 field mushrooms

2 tablespoons olive oil

½ teaspoon ground coriander

½ teaspoon ground cumin

2 cloves garlic

150g (5½ oz) pearl barley

2 tablespoons wine vinegar

3 tablespoons *nuoc mam* fish sauce

Take 3 carrots, 3 sticks of celery, 2 onions and half of the cabbage and chop roughly. Put in a large casserole with the chicken carcase and cover with the water. Add the bay leaves, cover, and boil for 2 hours over a very low heat. Strain the resulting stock, squeezing any juice out of the vegetables in a sieve, then set it aside.

Pour a bowlful of the hot stock over the porcini and leave them to stand for half an hour. When they are fully rehydrated, chop them into small pieces and return them and their soaking liquid to the rest of the stock.

Strip the rest of the celery of its strings and chop into small pieces. Chop the rest of the carrots, onions and mushrooms finely and shred the rest of the cabbage, then heat the olive oil in the casserole over a low heat. Add the carrots, cabbage, mushrooms, coriander, cumin and garlic, chopped, and fry for a couple of minutes, until they have softened slightly. Pour over the stock and add the pearl barley and celery. Bring to the boil and leave to simmer for 45 minutes. Stir in the wine vinegar and *nuoc mam* and garnish with the parsley before serving.

300

(Zack Snyder, 2006)

Antiquity was a bit like a gay disco – at least, that's the impression you get from watching *300*. The film recreates the ancient battle of Thermopylae as a death match between bulging-bicepped Spartan go-go boys and slinky Persian drag queens, all gyrating half-naked in a deafening, sweaty mass of bodies.

This is the back story: Leonidas (Gerard Butler) is ruler of the rugged, militaristic kingdom of Sparta. This is a place where weak babies are left to die and where boys are dragged from their mothers' arms at just seven years old to learn the cruel arts of war. The ones who make it back alive, however, are allowed to wear the garment that marks out the true Spartan warrior: an unfeasibly tiny pair of pants.

It's a tough life, but a good one – so Leonidas and his men are naturally peeved when emissaries from the Persian emperor turn up demanding their submission. Leonidas chucks the bejewelled and criminally unbutch messengers down a well in fury, and vows to save Sparta from the marauders. The problem is, not everyone is quite as gung-ho as he is. A few dove-like wimps in the Spartan senate have this lame faith in following the law, and doubt that the Persian army is quite the weapon of mass destruction Leonidas claims it is.

With a sneer at these quibbling pettifoggers, the king sets off with his three hundred best men, hoping to hold the vast Persian army back at the Hot Gates, a narrow ravine which offers a sneaky way into the body of Sparta. Thus starts an epic battle in which the tiny force of Spartan warriors tries to keep the Persian behemoth from lumbering up its stoutly defended back passage.

Though the Spartans are so massively outnumbered, it seems at first that their way of life is going to win out over the shifty dark-skinned Eastern aggressors, who – a murmured racist undertone, this – look rather like orcs escaped from Middle-earth. A pity, because although the Spartans are exceptionally skilled in the arts of shouting and posing, the Persians look like they have so much more fun. Their emperor Xerxes (Rodrigo Santoro) is a gorgeous seven-foot gender-bender encrusted with more gold and jewels than Donald Trump's guest bathroom. He surrounds himself with a bevy of beautiful and luxuriously clad freaks who writhe and squirm like a bucketful of eels whenever the camera is poked at them.

Sparta is dowdy by contrast – and they're always jabbering on about freedom even though, in real life, 85 per cent of Sparta's people were slaves – while Leonidas's spunky queen Gorgo (Lena Headey) has to dress herself in what look like a few strips of toilet paper. Still, Sparta's warriors certainly have a knack with their javelins, and it's only when a disabled traitor, guilty of the crime of being less than hunky, shows the Persians a way over the mountains that the bloody endgame begins.

Spartans were famous in antiquity for their frugal diet. Their staple food was 'black soup', a dubious concoction made with pig's blood. One ancient wag tried it and quipped that now he understood why Spartan warriors were so willing to die. This is my version, with the added luxury of asafoetida (see p. 264), the modern equivalent of the ancients' most favoured spice, *silphium*. If you are wary of, or unable to get, pig's blood, try using red wine mixed with a little soy sauce or *nuoc mam*.

Spartan Black Soup

2 onions	700ml (25 fl oz) water
2 leeks	2 bay leaves
4 cloves garlic	1 teaspoon oregano
2 tablespoons olive oil	½ teaspoon asafoetida
1 pork knuckle, bone in	large pinch of salt
1 pig's trotter	1 tablespoon coriander leaves,
500ml (17 fl oz) pig's blood	finely chopped
2 tablespoons red wine vinegar	

Chop the onions, leeks and garlic coarsely. Heat the oil over a low heat in a large casserole and cook the vegetables for a minute. Add the knuckle and trotter and brown briefly on all sides. Pour over the blood, vinegar and water and bring to the boil. Add the bay leaves, oregano and asafoetida and leave the soup to simmer for 2–3 hours. Strain the broth, and discard the vegetables. Strip the meat from the bone, chop it into very small pieces and return to the soup.

Add salt to taste, sprinkle with the coriander leaves and serve with mixed wheat and barley bread (available at health food stores).

Braveheart

(Mel Gibson, 1995)

Churning mud, torrential rain, cackling knights on horseback and lots of shouting – *Braveheart* certainly makes Scotland's Middle Ages look a bit glum. A race of unfeasibly hairy, dirt-caked hard cases who punch each other as a way of saying hello (and that's just the women), the Scots of Mel Gibson's medieval epic would have a pretty rough life even without the English menace constantly harrying them. But harry them they do. It's the thirteenth century and, with Scotland's throne left empty, the evil English king Edward Longshanks (Patrick McGoohan) has taken advantage of Scottish disunity to rampage through the country asserting his bloody lordship. Not content with mincing around triumphantly in gaudy orange singlets, the leering, subhuman English knights who arrive in Edward's wake also demand the right to bed any Scottish bride on her wedding night.

This would rile any upstanding Scot, but so far the film's hero, humble squireling William Wallace (Mel Gibson), claims rather unconvincingly to be a peace-loving man in search of a quiet life. We don't have to wait long, however, for the plot to furnish him with a personal motive for unleashing the massive cinematic bloodbath we've all been waiting for (which frees him up for more romantic shenanigans, to boot). A brutal English lord slits the throat of his young wife Murron (Catherine McCormack) for resisting rape, and Wallace vows to rid Scotland of the Sassenach scum who brought her low. Rallying the clansmen of Scotland against the English overlords, Wallace and his followers wipe the sneers off the English armies' faces at the battle of Stirling, striking terror into them with their blue body paint and chorus line of mooners.

King Edward is livid – not least because, while the renegade Wallace is a red-blooded ladies' man intent on piking any foe who comes near him, his son the Prince of Wales (Peter Hanly) treats his wife with revulsion and is only interested in burying his sword in his beloved companion Philip (Stephen Billington). The Prince's spurned wife, French princess Isabelle (Sophie Marceau), isn't really sure which side she's on, and becomes a pawn between the two countries when her father-in-law sends her to negotiate with Wallace.

As a little light relief is needed from the orgiastically gory battle scenes, Wallace falls in love with her – naturally enough, as she seems to be the first woman he's ever met who doesn't have filth smeared all over her face. This irregular liaison opens up a chink in the English armour, even though Wallace seems to be two-timing the French princess with the ghost of his dead wife. But with the high Scottish nobles still proving to be as effective as a battering ram made of haggis when it comes to uniting in rebellion, Scotland's future and Wallace's shaggy head are still poised on a knife edge.

This medieval Scottish recipe has a military origin that makes it the perfect tonic for a band of marauding men in skirts. Atholl Brose was first developed by the Earl of Atholl while fighting the Earl of Ross, Lord of the Isles. Apparently, Atholl filled a well his opponents were using with oatmeal, honey and whisky, and Ross's men became so heavy with drinking it that they were easily ambushed and captured. Admittedly this was a few years after William Wallace's time, so he probably didn't drink the stuff himself – but damn it, he didn't paint his face blue or even invade England in real life, so one more historical invention can hardly hurt.

Atholl Brose

25g (1 oz) porridge oats
250ml (8 fl oz) water

1 tbsp heather honey
250ml (8 fl oz) malt whisky

Put the oats in a large bowl and stir in the water. Mix thoroughly and leave to stand for 30 minutes. Place a fine sieve, ideally muslin, over another bowl and put in the soaked oats and their liquid. Press the oats with a spoon to strain as much liquid as you can from them and then throw them away, reserving their milky liquor. Add the honey to the liquid and stir until fully dissolved. Mix in the whisky, then pour into four glasses. If you like, the brose can be poured into a bottle (or, better, a hip flask) and kept for later, though as the drink has a tendency to separate, it will need a good shake.

An ideal companion on a long walk, or if you need a bit of extra pep in mid-battle.

american
indie

Reservoir Dogs

(Quentin Tarantino, 1992)

If you had to drink a shot every time someone in *Reservoir Dogs* said 'f***', you'd be in A&E having your stomach pumped before Mr White (Harvey Keitel) had finished his first cigarette. He's part of a potty-mouthed gang put together by gangster Joe Cabot (Lawrence Tierney) to stick up a diamond wholesalers on rock delivery day. Dressed to kill in black suits and ties, it's as if they already know they're on their way to their own funerals. Sure enough, despite planning everything down to the last detail, the heist goes down the U-bend when the cops turn up sooner than expected. Shooting their way out of the shop leaving a daisy chain of stiffs behind them, the gang regroup at an abandoned warehouse to work out which one wised the police up to their plans.

On second glance, the code-named team are an unlikely bunch. Mr Pink (Steve Buscemi) is a weasel-faced tightwad who won't tip a waitress on principle, while Mr Blonde (Michael Madsen) turns out to be a trigger-happy psycho-path whose fondness for middle-of-the-road 70s folk-rock is as gruesome as his habit of ripping ears off with a switch-blade. Mr Brown (Quentin Tarantino) is convinced that all Madonna's most anodyne hits are about bitter, excruciating sex, and Mr Orange (Tim Roth) is a bundle of nerves who panics like a child on a ghost train the moment a bullet hits him.

It's Mr White who mostly holds things together – that is, until Mr Pink suggests that a rat in their midst has set them all up. With half the gang dead or bleeding, and the other half trusting no one, time may be running out. Will they manage to find the grass they suspect of tipping off the police, or will they lose their cool first and create a Jackson Pollock-style mural all over the warehouse's walls with each other's brains instead?

Reservoir Dogs might not be the best movie to enjoy with a quiet dinner, but this recipe still makes an excellent pairing. Why? Because it's a f***ing piece of meat torn to f***ing shreds then served up raw, that's why, asshole. And just like the film, while it might sound disgusting on paper, it's actually a classic.

Steak Tartare

700g (1 lb 9 oz) steak, either fillet
   or T-bone
4 baby gherkins
1 tablespoon capers
1 dash Tabasco sauce
1 teaspoon Worcester Sauce
½ teaspoon Dijon mustard
   (optional)

2 shallots
1 handful flat-leaf parsley
2 egg yolks, as fresh as you can
   get
1 tablespoon olive oil
salt and pepper
4 lettuce leaves

Trim any bones from the meat, which must be lean, extremely fresh and of the best quality. Using a sharp knife, cut the meat into very thin slivers. Cut these slivers into tiny dice and return to the fridge to cool. Chop the gherkins, capers, shallots and parsley very finely. Beat the egg yolks, then add the Tabasco and Worcester sauces, the mustard, oil, salt and pepper to taste, and whip until light and fluffy. Blend all the ingredients with the chilled meat very thoroughly, then divide into 4 teacups. Flatten the meat in the cups to form a dense cake, then turn them out on to the lettuce leaves.

The steak can be briefly re-chilled, but should not be prepared more than 2 hours before serving.

Short Cuts

(Robert Altman, 1993)

No one should let a dead body in the water spoil a good day's fishing. At least, that's what Stuart Kane (Fred Ward) and his fishing buddies think. They've just pitched camp by a damn fine trout stream in the Southern California wilds when they notice the corpse of a young woman bobbing up and down. Rather than ruin their trip, they decide to tether her to the bank and contact the law only once they've bagged a few good ones. Such shifty behaviour is typical of the ragbag of compromised, neither good nor evil characters in Robert Altman's film. Citizens of a sprawling Los Angeles, all that seems to link them are the planes spraying bug killer that are slowly poisoning them all as they strafe the city. Nonetheless, we soon learn that the whole cast are connected in a way that only characters in an ambitious arty movie can ever be.

But how? Working out the relationships between the storylines in this superb Raymond Carver adaptation is as straightforward as flying to the moon in a rocket made of soup. We could start with careworn diner waitress Doreen (Lily Tomlin), who is trying to shake some sense into her deadbeat husband – Tom Waits, with a face like an ageing basset hound, in a perfect bit of casting as a messed-up alcoholic.

When a little boy runs into Doreen's car on her way home from work, she little knows it will lead to his parents being tormented by a disgruntled cake decorator (well you wouldn't, would you?). These parents, in turn, have no idea that their chunky pool cleaner Jerry (Chris Penn) is being driven nuts by his sex-line worker wife moaning over the phone for sticky-digited heavy breathers while she's changing nappies. And while artist Marian Wyman (Julianne Moore) is quarrelling about past infidelities with her husband, stripped from the waist down (clearly she didn't see the camera crew in the corner of the room), she doesn't know that the fish they're going to eat for dinner has been swimming around a cadaver.

That's right – Stuart Kane, the cold-hearted fisherman we met earlier, is bringing his wife and the weekend's catch over for dinner with their new friends – how's that for a twist? And did I mention that Stuart's wife Claire (Anne Archer) is the birthday clown? And that she gets chatted up by a dodgy cop (Tim Robbins) who's cheating on his wife Sherri (Madeleine Stowe)? And that Sherri is best friends with Marian, the dinner-party hostess walking around with her privates on parade? Are you still with me? As seismic rumbles flatten the characters to the ground near the film's end, it's hard to be sure if it's an earthquake or the force of the screenwriter's head exploding.

With LA being so close to Mexico, Hispanic flavours (such as this adobo sauce) have almost taken over the city's cuisine, hence this spicy way of serving the grilled trout that feature so prominently in *Short Cut*'s storyline. Don't be overly alarmed by the amount of chillies: the dried ones are relatively mild. And as there are lots of parts to this dish, the sauces can be kept in the fridge and used for other meals.

Adobo Marinated Trout with Corn Salsa

For the adobo sauce

4 ancho chillies

4 guajillo chillies (see p. 265)

oil

500ml (17 fl oz) boiling water

1 tablespoon tomato purée

1 onion, chopped

2 cloves garlic, chopped

1 teaspoon cumin

½ teaspoon dried oregano

¼ teaspoon salt

juice of 4 limes

1 teaspoon cornflour

For the corn salsa

4 corn cobs

6 tomatoes

1 green chilli, finely chopped

2 red onions, finely chopped

2 heaped tablespoons coriander, finely chopped

juice of 2 lemons

AMERICAN INDIE

The trout

4 trout, gutted, washed and dried   2 cloves garlic, minced
Juice of 2 limes   salt

Start with the adobo sauce. Cut the tops off the chillies and scoop out the seeds. In a saucepan fry the chillies in hot oil for 5 minutes. Remove from the heat, cover with the boiling water and leave for 4 hours, or overnight. Drain, then put the chillies in a blender with the tomato purée and half the soaking liquid (throw the rest away) and blend to a thin pulp. Soften the onion and garlic in a pan in a little more oil. Pour the liquid into the pan and bring to the boil. Add the cumin, oregano, salt and lime juice. Sieve in the cornflour, stirring all the time, and boil the sauce until it is thick but still easy to pour. Put into a jar and store for later use.

Then the corn salsa. Grill the corn cobs, if possible over charcoal, until brown. Take a small knife and, holding the kernels by one end, scrape the knife down them (away from you) to strip off the corn. Cut a little cross on the skin of each tomato, cover them with boiling water for 30 seconds, then drain and peel. Chop them finely, then mix with the other ingredients.

Finally the trout. Sprinkle their skins with salt. Smear the insides with the lime juice, minced garlic and a tablespoon of the adobo sauce. Leave to stand for half an hour. Grill, ideally over charcoal, for 4 minutes per side (the lime juice will already have partially cured the flesh).

Serve with the corn salsa, plus rice and a green salad.

Blue Velvet

(David Lynch, 1986)

'Do you like to do bad things?' asks sultry nightclub singer
Dorothy Vallens (Isabella Rossellini) as she rubs herself up
against geeky student Jeffrey Beaumont (Kyle MacLachlan).
Seeing that he has already picked up a human ear as a keepsake,
stolen Dorothy's keys, broken into her apartment and watched
her while she undresses, the answer is probably yes. Still, his
peeping Tom antics have revealed rather more than he bar-
gained for, as he has inadvertently stepped into a nightmare
world of child kidnapping, fabric fetishism and inept Roy Orbi-
son lip-synching. Breaking in because he suspected Dorothy
of being connected to the severed ear (not literally, of course),
Jeffrey has been caught by her and forced to strip at knife-
point as a punishment. She then suddenly hustles him into a
cupboard as brutal hood Frank Booth (Dennis Hopper) enters.

With a gas mask full of helium clamped to his face, a
tendency to lash out at any moment and a strip of fetishistic
blue velvet forever twisting around his fingers, Frank isn't
exactly the sort of person you'd invite to a children's party or
ask to look after a kitten. But he has an unexplained power
over Dorothy, whom he forces into gruesome sex, clad in the
blue velvet robe that so excites him, alternately calling her
'Bitch!' and 'Mommy!'

Jeffrey comforts her when Frank leaves, but things are about to take a yet darker turn that even the apple-pie sweetness of Jeffrey's wholesome blonde neighbour and helper Sandy Williams (Laura Dern) can't lighten. What's more, the glossy unreality of the film has left so many things unexplained. Can Jeffrey find a way to break Frank's steely grip on Dorothy? Why does a church organ play on the soundtrack whenever winsome Sandy speaks? And how does Dorothy make any money as a performer with a singing voice like Marge Simpson with laryngitis?

Lookswise, this velvety-textured dessert is about as Gothic as it gets, though you can push the boat out even further by adding blue colouring if you wish. If you have an artistic hand and a strong stomach, might I suggest fashioning an ear from marzipan and food colouring to go with each portion?

Blueberry Velvet

600g (21 oz) blueberries
400ml (14 fl oz) water
juice of 2 lemons
400g (14 oz) sweetened
condensed milk

20g (¾ oz) gelatine
1 teacup water, not quite boiling
3½ tablespoons sugar
single cream for serving

Put 500g (18 oz) of the blueberries in a blender and blend to a smooth pulp. Rub the pulp through a fine sieve to remove any larger pieces of skin, then dilute this juice with 200ml (7 fl oz) of the water and the juice of 1 lemon. Empty the condensed milk into a large bowl and whip the blueberry and lemon juice into it very gradually. (If you do this all at once, you run the risk of curdling the milk.) Dissolve the gelatine in the hot water. Once it has cooled to lukewarmth, stir into the blueberry milk. Pour the mixture into a mould and leave in a cool place to set thoroughly for at least 4 hours.

Meanwhile, pulp the remaining blueberries in the blender, rub through a sieve and put in a saucepan with the remaining water and lemon juice. Add the sugar and bring the pan to the boil. Once the sugar has dissolved, boil the liquid down by about half to produce a rich, viscous syrup. Leave this to cool thoroughly. When you are ready to eat, turn out the mould and pour the syrup over the dessert.

Serve with the single cream.

To Die For

(Gus Van Sant, 1995)

How far would you go to be on television? Wannabe presenter Suzanne Stone (Nicole Kidman) is prepared to claw, suck and even kill to get on the box, if that's what it takes.

She's so determined to make it that she secretly plans her honeymoon to coincide with a TV producers' conference in Florida. While Larry Maretto (Matt Dillon), her hunky lump of a husband, is out fishing, she's humping crinkly TV execs in the hope of getting a break. Luckily for her, Suzanne possesses many of the ideal anchor-person's qualities: clean-cut WASP good looks, pearly teeth and an upbeat manner so grindingly chipper she's almost begging for a rotten tomato to land in her kisser. Unluckily, despite her devious grit, she's lacking a major component of the full package: the brains to back up her brute ambition. While she manages to hook a weather girl job at her sleepy New England hometown's teensy cable station, her half-baked plans to reach superstardom and ditch her husband in the process prove to be as watertight as a chocolate teapot.

Fishing around for programme ideas which she can bully her apathetic bosses into screening, she sets up a project interviewing teens at a local high school about their lives. No matter that the pupils who sign up are a bunch of imbecilic, giggling wasters whose greatest ambitions are to get stoned or have sex with Motley Crue. She sits up night after night editing their brainless dronings like they were fragments of the Dead Sea Scrolls. Back at home, it becomes clear pretty soon that her husband's hopes and hers won't mesh. While he wants kids and thinks getting artificial plants for his family's Italian restaurant is a bold step forward, she won't stop until millions all over America are switching channels to avoid her. So how can she use her new-found teen connections to loosen her family ties? Slowly a cunning if precarious plan starts forming in Suzanne's head . . .

On the surface, Suzanne Stone is every bit as wholesome as a freshly baked apple pie; this version adds another appropriately New Englandy ingredient, cranberries, to create something a little sharper. Just like Suzanne, while this pie looks sugar-sweet and innocent on the outside, on first bite you'll find that it's actually a little tart.

Cranberry and Apple Pie

175g (6½ oz) plain flour	40g (1½ oz) lard
½ teaspoon salt	40g (1½ oz) butter

AMERICAN INDIE

water

400g (14 oz) cooking apples,
   peeled and cored

200g (7½ oz) cranberries

130g (5 oz) granulated sugar

1½ extra tablespoons flour

1 tablespoon lemon juice

½ teaspoon ground cinnamon

milk

Sieve the flour and salt into a bowl. Cut the fats into small cubes and add to the bowl. Rub the fats into the flour, until you have a crumb-like mixture. Make a well in the centre and add about 2 tablespoons of cold water. Stir in with a knife to make a soft pastry; then, using your hands, form into a single ball. The pastry should no longer stick to the bowl. If it does, add a drop more water. Cover with cling film and leave to rest in the fridge.

Thirty minutes later, roll the pastry out thinly, and trace a lid out of it by pressing the top of the pie dish on to it, then cutting around the outline. Re-roll the remaining pastry, and use it to line the pie dish.

Slice the apples thinly and roughly chop the cranberries. Mix the fruit in a bowl with the sugar, the extra flour, the lemon juice and cinnamon until well coated. Fill this pastry with this filling, patting it down evenly, then put the lid on top. Press the two edges together firmly to seal, pinching around the resulting edge in little flutes. Cut a little hole in the centre of the pie to let any steam out, then brush the top with a little milk and dust lightly with more sugar. Bake the pie in an oven preheated to 200°C/400°F/Mark 6 for 30 minutes.

Serve warm with cream.

Boogie Nights

(Paul Thomas Anderson, 1997)

'I just know there's somethin' wonderful under those jeans just waitin' to get out,' says suave crinkly faced porn producer Jack Horner (Burt Reynolds). Indeed Dirk Diggler (Mark Wahlberg), the man he's talking to, proves to be blessed with a todger so mammoth it looks like a baby's arm holding an apple. Dirk is a bit of a humanitarian and realizes that, with his endowment, it's his duty to share with the world his glorious gift for getting it on.

Working as a busboy and part-time hustler in a San Fernando Valley disco in the late 70s, Dirk stumbles across Horner one night. Sensing the colossal talent hidden in Diggler's trousers, Horner reckons he could thereby pump some much needed new blood into his films and beat off the stiff competition. So Dirk moves into Horner's house and enters a strange new shiny world, where garish nylon is the height of chic, people live caked in cocaine like cod in batter, and calling a woman 'the foxiest bitch' is a sweet, thoughtful compliment. He and his fellow stars live like a little family. Rollergirl (Heather Graham), a pretty young nymphet fresh from high school, is the baby, while everyone rests their heads on the welcoming bosom of mother hen Amber Waves (Julianne Moore) – that is, when they're not shooting all over it on camera.

Diggler's career goes off with a bang. Teaming up with sidekick Reed Rothchild (John C. Reilly), he wins a string of industry awards in the role of Brock Landers, an international karate-kicking, ho-slapping spy and stud whose performances are wooden in more ways than one. But with an increasing drug habit depleting the blood supply to his money-maker, sweet-natured Dirk is turning bitter and his efforts are flagging. Furious, he becomes paranoid when he sees Horner employing new meat, so he storms out and tries to set himself up as a rock vocalist of the rasping, grunting, air-punching variety. But with the glory days of the porn film giving way to shabby video, and cheapo bump 'n' grind merchants taking over from the porn aristocracy of the 70s, Dirk finds that he is increasingly spilling his seed on barren ground.

This summery Californian cocktail is a great way of taking champagne and making it taste like alcoholic soda pop. As Diggler and co., stars of the odd cock-tale themselves (forgive me), are fans of conspicuous consumption but not razor-sharp in the taste department, it suits them to a T. Of course, you could cut corners by using Cava, but that just wouldn't be, y'know, foxy.

California Dreamin' Cocktail

1 lemon	300ml (10 fl oz) pineapple juice
100ml (4 fl oz) kirschwasser	1 round of pineapple, skin left on
(or vodka)	½ bottle champagne
8 ice cubes	

Plus

a lemon zester

Using a zester, peel 4 spirals of zest off the lemon (if you have no zester, you could try with a sharp knife, but it's decidedly tricky). Set the zest aside and squeeze the juice out of the lemon. Put the kirschwasser, ice, pineapple juice and lemon juice in a blender and blend thoroughly. Divide the drink between four 250ml (8 fl oz) wine glasses and add a lemon twist to each. Quarter the pineapple slice and cut a slit halfway up each piece. Slide these on to the rim of each glass. Top up with the champagne and serve immediately.

Snow White and the Seven Dwarfs

(Walt Disney, 1937)

Most of us are familiar with the story of Snow White, the sugary, innocent young princess driven from her home by a jealous stepmother. But looking at Disney's cartoon I can't help wondering if she's really all that different from her father's wicked new wife. Certainly, she doesn't spend her life bickering with a chatty mirror as her guardian does, but when she's turned loose in the forest after she's been spotted flirting with a passing prince, Snow White soon acts in ways that are scarcely less witchy.

First, she appears to have the gift of summoning the beasts of the dark woods and ordering them to attend to her every whim. She may well be rather cute with her puffed sleeves and little piglet voice, but I wouldn't feel entirely safe around a woman with the power to compel floppy-eared bunnies to do the washing-up.

Then there's the breaking and entering. When she finds the Seven Dwarfs' lair, she swans in and takes possession immediately, spread-eagling herself all over their beds and leaving the little men to cower sootily around the kitchen hearth like seven hairy miniature Cinderellas. Admittedly, the hovel of seven drooling old men wallowing in their own filth might not seem that appealing, but then a girl turned out of her home for flagrant vamping of any passing prince can't be too choosy, can she?

Still, she *is* a great beauty. With lips as red as ketchup, hair as black as tarmac and skin as creamy as the head on a pint of Guinness, there's more than a touch of the teenage Goth to young Snow White. And when her stepmother finally tracks her down and plays up to her gluttony by offering her a noxious apple, her charms remain quite unwithered as she lies in the glass casket her dwarfs have prepared for her. It isn't until a prince with necrophiliac tendencies comes riding by and can't resist copping a feel of the gorgeous stiff that the blood returns to her cheeks, and they all live happily ever . . .

As we all know, Snow White was laid low by fruit steeped in poison. This is my version of the wicked queen's apples. Coated in a dark layer of brittle liquorice toffee, they are probably the most evil-looking confectionery you'll ever see.

Liquorice Toffee Apples

110ml (4 fl oz) water
40g (1½ oz) liquorice sticks, finely chopped

200g (7½ oz) soft brown sugar
1 tablespoon treacle
1 tablespoon Golden Syrup

ANIMATION

30g (1 oz) butter 4 sweet apples
½ teaspoon wine vinegar

Plus

a sugar thermometer
4 wooden chopsticks

Heat the water in a saucepan. Add the liquorice and dissolve it over a very gentle heat – the liquorice will need regular prodding with a spoon to encourage it to dissolve. Once all the lumps have disappeared, add the sugar and stir until it dissolves. Then stir in the treacle, Golden Syrup, butter and vinegar and bring to the boil.

Testing the temperature with a sugar thermometer, boil the syrup until it reaches the hard-crack phase (146–154°C/294–309°F). Be careful not to put the syrup on too high a flame and burn it (its temperature will go up automatically as its water content reduces, so high heat isn't necessary). Gauging when you've reached the hard stage is rather difficult if you don't have a thermometer, but you can also test by dropping a drop of the toffee syrup into a glass of cold water – when the droplet forms a ball that cracks on contact with the water, the syrup is ready.

While the syrup is boiling, wash and dry the apples and make a little incision at each core's base with a knife or skewer. Thrust a chopstick into the centre of each apple. When the syrup is ready, dip each apple in it, leave to harden for a few moments, then dip again. Repeat the process until you have a thick layer covering the whole fruit. Leave to stand (vertical, fruit down) on a greased baking sheet until the liquorice toffee coating has fully hardened.

Shrek

(Andrew Adamson/Vicky Jenson, 2001)

Fairytales aren't what they used to be, as distressed damsel Princess Fiona learns when she gets rescued after years of incarceration. The princess (voiced by Cameron Diaz) has been languishing in a high tower waiting for Prince Charming to free her from a dragon and awaken her with love's first kiss. But instead of the dashing, chiselled knight errant she was expecting, she gets gruff, insect-guzzling Scottish ogre Shrek (Mike Myers), who looks like a cross between Wayne Rooney and the Incredible Hulk.

Mind you, Shrek isn't that keen to be there either. The only reason he's agreed to rescue the swooning princess is because the diminutive tyrant of Duloc, Lord Farquaad (John Lithgow), has evicted all fairytale characters from his perfect realm and forced them to flee into Shrek's swamp. With the wolf from *Red Riding Hood* snoring in his bed and the Seven Dwarfs dumping snoozing Snow White on his kitchen table, Shrek has no option but to journey to Duloc's spookily pristine toytown to sort things out.

There the demented control freak Farquaad (a sly caricature of Walt Disney himself, perhaps?) needs to marry a princess if he wants to become a king. He agrees to let Shrek's squatters have their land back on one condition: that

Shrek rescues Princess Fiona and brings her back to marry him.

So off Shrek goes, but as no questing knight is complete without his noble steed, he grudgingly brings along comedy sidekick Donkey (Eddie Murphy). Together the pair rescue the bemused and ungrateful princess and start retracing their steps back to Duloc. But despite being at first disappointed in each other, a rapport slowly develops between Shrek and his troublesome royal trophy. With their mutual fondness for fighting, belching and feasting on insects, could the potato-headed Shrek and the luscious, svelte Fiona have more in common than they realize?

There's little that Shrek appears to enjoy more than a plateful of fat grubs or flies – that is, when no fish eyes are to be had. If you fancy trying some of his diet but don't have a handy swamp to gather the ingredients from, this recipe makes an excellent substitute. Generations of children have complained that tapioca, the once popular nursery pudding, looks exactly like frogspawn. Well, this creamy coconut pudding makes a virtue of that, producing a comforting but delicate dessert that also happens to look like a cluster of amphibian larvae.

Coconut Frogspawn

80g (3 oz) large tapioca pearls
   (see p. 269)
500ml (17 fl oz) milk *or* 400ml
   (14 fl oz) milk plus 100ml
   (4 fl oz) single cream
1 tablespoon creamed coconut
200ml (7 fl oz) coconut milk

100g (4 oz) granulated sugar
1 tablespoon desiccated coconut
1 tablespoon pomegranate seeds
   (optional – their sharpness
   provides a nice contrast,
   though)

Mix the tapioca with the milk, cream (if you're using it), creamed coconut and coconut milk in a large saucepan and bring gently to the boil, stirring throughout. Keep the pan on the lowest simmer possible and stir in the sugar gradually. Boil the tapioca pearls until nearly cooked through, stirring every two minutes or so. This process usually takes 25–30 minutes, but if your pearls have been sitting on a shelf for a long time, it may take up to 45. You can tell they are cooked when most of them have turned translucent, and there is only a small trace of white remaining inside the jelly of each. When you reach this stage, remove the pan from the heat, stir one last time and leave covered for 30 minutes.

When it has cooled, stir in the desiccated coconut. You will be left with a creamy white custard filled with what look like lots of baby eggs. This can either be eaten warm or left to chill fully.

For serving, spoon the pudding into 4 dessert glasses and sprinkle a teaspoonful of pomegranate seeds on top of each one.

Spirited Away

(Hayao Miyazaki, 2001)

Don't humans make your stomach turn? The food they eat makes them stink so badly you can smell them a mile off. That's what the supernatural beings in Miyazaki's psychedelically inventive *Spirited Away* think, anyway. When a little girl called Chihiro stumbles accidentally into their world, the human stench she carries means that everyone knows there is an unwelcome intruder in their midst – but how on earth did she get there?

It all started when Chihiro and her parents came across what they thought was an abandoned theme park. Discovering an unattended stall piled high with succulent food, her parents greedily stuffed themselves. Chihiro refused to join them, though, and watched in horror as they turned into enormous snarfing pigs. For this was no theme park. The family had inadvertently strayed into a giant bathhouse where the Shinto spirits of living objects – plants, animals, even vegetables – come for a break from their duties in the human world, to eat well and soak their weary limbs in herbal hot tubs. Chihiro's guzzling parents had been punished for stealing food intended for the spirits, and were now in serious danger of being turned into bacon themselves.

Receiving protection from a boy called Haku, Chihiro

learns that the only way she will be allowed to stay at the bathhouse long enough to rescue her parents is to find a job there. Otherwise the bathhouse's magical owner Yubaba – a sort of hideously magnified Oompa-Loompa with a wart the size of a football and a granny hairstyle larger than your average pony – will turn her into a lump of coal. Chihiro is terrified by the spirit world she has entered. But this is only the very beginning of her mind-bending adventures, where she will be helped on her way by enchanted lumps of soot, work for a friendly old spider, become best friends with a river and share a lift with the spirit of a radish.

There's something strangely bulimic about *Spirited Away*. When characters aren't stuffing their faces, they're vomiting – and feeling much the better for it. This recipe is for a classic and extremely popular type of Japanese rice cake – we see Chihiro being given one of these by her workmate and helper Lin. As they have a springy, chewy consistency, you may find that one or two are quite satisfying enough. Just remember to keep them down.

ANIMATION

Japanese Rice and Bean Cakes (Daifuku)

For the bean stuffing

200g (7½ oz) aduki beans
2¼ litres (4⅕ pints) water
pinch of salt
200g (7½ oz) brown sugar
    (I prefer brown sugar, but
    use white if you wish)

15g (¼ oz) of raisins (optional –
    and not strictly authentic)

For the cakes

120g (4½ oz) rice flour
40g (1½ oz) icing sugar
120ml (4½ fl oz) water

2 tablespoons potato flour for
    dusting (not essential, but it
    makes them less sticky)

Plus

greaseproof paper

Start with the stuffing. Soak the aduki beans overnight in water, then drain them. Bring ¾ litre (27 fl oz) of water to the boil and add the beans. When they have returned to the boil, drain the beans and discard the water. Boil another 1½ litres (2½ pints) of water with a pinch of salt and return the beans to the pan. Once they have boiled, reduce the heat to a low simmer and cook for an hour. Add the sugar and stir until dissolved, then remove from the heat. If you are using raisins, add them now.

By this time, the beans should have disintegrated slightly into the water, creating a loose paste. As the paste cools, mash and stir the beans into their syrup to create a thick paste. It needs to be thick enough to act as a stuffing, but don't worry about making it entirely smooth. When it has cooled enough to put your finger in, take the stuffing out a teaspoonful at a time and drop on to a tray lined with greaseproof or waxed paper. Taking them into your palm, roll each spoonful into a little ball. Put the tray in a cool place, ideally the freezer, and leave for 20 minutes.

Now for the cakes. Mix the flour, sugar and water in a saucepan, making sure no lumps remain. Heat the pan over a medium flame, stirring constantly. After a few minutes, the mixture will start to thicken. When it comes away from the sides of the pan in one lump and is slightly hard to stir, pour and spoon it on to a well-floured surface, spreading out thinly and evenly with a spatula. Fill the pan with hot water and leave to soak – dried-on rice flour is hard to dislodge.

You are aiming to make about 9 cakes, so you can measure if you have the correct thinness by seeing how many times a biscuit cutter or glass tumbler will fit over the sheet of dough. Leave it to cool until it's comfortable to hold in your hand, then cut it into circles using the cutter or tumbler. Dust your hands well with flour. Then take a circle in your hand, place a ball of the chilled stuffing on it and fold the dough over the ball. Squeeze shut, then pat into a round shape (this is easier than it sounds – trust me). Dust the cakes with the potato flour and leave for 10 minutes, to let the stuffing thaw – the cakes need no more cooking.

Serve with Japanese tea.

Brokeback Mountain

(Ang Lee, 2005)

Beans, beans, beans. That's all lonesome sheepboys Jack Twist (Jake Gyllenhaal) and Ennis Del Mar (Heath Ledger) get to eat, day in, day out. Stuck in the photogenic wilds of Wyoming's Brokeback Mountain, the two handsome shepherds have been hired for the summer to tend a flock grazing on the high pasture. Though they get on well enough, they make a pretty unlikely duo: while Jack is a prancing, half-punch-drunk rodeo cowboy, Ennis is a mumbling introvert who chews on any word of more than one syllable as if it were an exceedingly sticky toffee. Their days filled with shooing away coyotes and shoving down their unvarying diet, it can be a pretty tough life. Still, 1960s Wyoming is a pretty tough place, where herding livestock seems to be the only job going and every man looks as if he moonlights as a member of the Village People.

To break the dietary tedium in camp, the pair decide to bulk out their rations with their rifles. Ennis downs an elk, so they spend the night in front of the fire gorging themselves on fresh meat. It soon transpires that elk isn't the only meat on the night's menu. Weighed down with flesh and whisky, Ennis is too weary to ride back up to his night watch higher in the pastures, so he and Jack end up sharing the tent.

Huddling together in the freezing night, the unspoken truth that's been hanging in the air for some time suddenly comes out in the open: Jack and Ennis have fallen in love. They then have sex for the first time (at least, I think they do – they're so rough that at first glance you'd think they were wrestling steer).

Alas, the summer ends all too soon and the shepherds have to head on back to their homes, kissing each other farewell with a goodbye punch. In a world where admitting you're gay is as taboo as confessing to a fondness for mating with dead raccoons, there's no place where Jack and Ennis's love can thrive. But even though they both furnish themselves with wives and kids, neither can shake off the memories of their sheep-worrying, wildlife-shooting days back up on Brokeback.

What follows is a slightly fancier version of what Jack and Ennis ate out in the wilds (something tells me that they probably didn't have cinnamon). If you want to stick to the film's story, you could try serving this dish of elk and beans with the duo's favourite accompaniment – beans.

Elk and Bean Stew

100g (4 oz) dried haricot beans,
    soaked overnight
2 medium onions
6 carrots
4 tomatoes
2 apples
splash of oil
50g (2 oz) butter
500g (18 oz) elk meat
    (or venison), cubed
500ml (18 fl oz) dark ale,
    such as Newcastle Brown
    or McEwan's

500ml (18 fl oz) vegetable stock
2 teaspoons Golden Syrup
1 teaspoon thyme
1 teaspoon rosemary
2 bayleaves
¼ teaspoon cinnamon
1 tablespoon plain flour
salt and pepper

Boil the beans in water for 30 minutes, then drain and discard the cooking liquid. While they are cooking, peel and dice the onions and carrots. Scratch a little cross with the tip of a knife in each tomato and cover them with boiling water. Leave them for 30 seconds, then drain them, slip off the skins and chop the tomatoes roughly. Peel and core the apples and chop the flesh into small chunks.

Put the oil in a large casserole, then melt the butter in it over a low heat. Fry the vegetables and apple for a couple of minutes, then add the meat. Cook until it has taken colour on all sides. Pour over the beer and stock, stir in the partially cooked beans and add all the remaining ingredients, stirring in the flour carefully so as not to form lumps. Season and simmer gently until the beans and meat are tender – at least 90 minutes (older beans can take longer) – adding more liquid if necessary.

Serves 4 with bread or potatoes.

Bound

(Andy and Larry Wachowski, 1996)

There may be some truth in the cliché about lesbians preferring their fingernails short, but mobster Caesar (Joe Pantoliano) is maybe taking things a little too far when he threatens to trim his girlfriend Violet's (Jennifer Tilly) right down to the knuckle with a wire-cutter.

You can see why he's angry with her, though. Despite playing the role of simpering, submissive moll to perfection, vampish Violet is secretly up to her elbows in love with ex-con dyke handywoman Corky (Gina Gershon), who is fixing up the apartment next door. With lithe tattooed limbs and lips so lusciously pouty she doesn't appear able to shut them, Corky reaches the parts of Violet that Caesar didn't even know existed, as Violet discovers when she invites her round to fiddle with her plumbing. Wanting to split while she's running, Violet has decided she's had enough of doing the dirty with the mob and thinks Corky might help her find a way out of her lushly upholstered but grim confinement.

The couple's big chance comes when the mob discovers one of their members has skimmed 2 million dollars off the business. Caesar has always worked as a money launderer, so it's only fitting that when the secret hoard is discovered he's responsible for bringing it home, washing all the embezzler's blood off and ironing it crisp again. Violet knows that Caesar loathes the boss's son, hot-headed psycho Johnnie (Christopher Meloni), and will immediately blame him if the dosh goes walkies. So while she creates a diversion, Corky creeps in from next door, steals the money and fills the case with yesterday's papers.

The ruse works, but are the lovers really smart enough to take on the mob? If they are, then why do they do things as monumentally stupid as chatting on the phone about what they're up to while Caesar is in the next room? With half America's wise guys due at the apartment, will Violet's faux innocence keep Caesar off her trail for long enough, or have she and Corky stuck their fingers in a pie that's far too hot for them?

In a nod to the wire-cutters that crop up throughout the story, this recipe is an intense version of a layered barbed-wire cocktail, cut through with the extra sharpness of a dash of lime.

GAY AND LESBIAN

Wire-cutter Cocktail

1 lime
salt
60ml (2½ fl oz) Campari

60ml (2½ fl oz) Curaçao-type
orange liqueur (Cointreau,
Grand Marnier, Triple Sec)
60ml (2½ fl oz) kirschwasser

Plus

4 shot-glasses

Quarter the lime and rub the rims of the glasses with a segment each. Scatter a thin layer of salt over a saucer and twist each glass in it so as to coat the rim. Squeeze the remaining juice from the lime quarters and spoon carefully into the glasses, taking care not to dislodge the salt. Pour 15ml (two large teaspoons) of Campari into each glass. Hold a spoon with its bowl facing upwards in each glass, one by one, and carefully pour over first the orange liqueur, then the kirschwasser. Take care not to do this too roughly, as you want to get a layered effect, with the clear ingredients floating on top of the Campari.

The Adventures of Priscilla, Queen of the Desert

(Stephan Elliott, 1994)

Has veteran drag queen Tick Belrose/Mitzi Del Bra (Hugo Weaving) lost it? It seems Sydney's gay pubs are getting bored with his skewed wigs, underpowered dance routines and off-cue lip-synching.

Deciding to shake off the cobwebs with a trip out of town, he accepts a four-week gig in Alice Springs, nestling far away in the arid outback like a tiny spot of mould in the centre of a dry cracker. Putting together a drag trio, he pairs up with old friend Bernadette Bassenger (Terence Stamp), a statuesque transsexual who bears a striking resemblance to a male actor of the 1960s. As Bernadette's lover has just died of asphyxiation from his own peroxide, she agrees to come along just so as to wash him out of her hair. Unfortunately, you need three for a trio – so Tick and Bernadette unwillingly enlist Adam/Felicia (Guy Pearce), an ear-splittingly shrill, acid-tongued young bitch with all the tact and understatement of an angry bullock trapped in a Balenciaga ballgown.

In the interests of plot, the threesome don't fly (in-flight air-conditioning can wilt a wig in minutes), but instead rustle up 10,000 Aussie dollars and buy a bloody great bus. With the axles groaning under their cargo of falsies, feathers and gin, they're ready for the outback. But is the outback ready for them? Well, the trip would run as smooth as Kylie Minogue's Brazilian-waxed inside leg if it wasn't for some of those belching, perverted alcoholics they run into on the way – women, I believe they call them. One tries to get them thrown out of a bar, quite brazenly showing her makeupless face without so much as a feather boa to set off her rugged complexion. Another, a former Thai stripper, upstages their act by catapulting ping-pong balls out of her unmentionables and speaks in a demented stereotypical East Asian pidgin even more grating than Felicia's screech.

But it's when Felicia unwisely pops a pill and tries to cruise some miners that it fully dawns on the three that they're not in Kansas any more. Does the Australian outback really have a place in its heart for three drag queens who mouth song lyrics for a living while tottering around like a trio of drunken flamingos? It's only when they reach Alice Springs that Tick's real motivation for the trip becomes apparent. With some unexpected family responsibilities creeping back out of the firmly shut closet of his past life, he has to ask himself whether, while he may be good at mouthing Abba, he is woman enough to be a man.

Daiquiris, we learn, are Tick's favourite tipple, despite his claims to be sick to the back teeth of them. As a rich but refreshing tropical version of a classic Cuban drink, this pulpy cocktail is almost thick enough to eat with a spoon.

PULP KITCHEN

Mango Daiquiris

4 large ripe mangoes
200ml (7 fl oz) white rum
50ml (2 fl oz) orange liqueur (e.g
   Curaçao, Cointreau or Grand
   Marnier)

juice of 4 limes
2–4 teaspoons icing sugar
   (optional, according to taste)
10 large ice cubes

Cut each mango, with the skin still on, into three large crossways slices, with the central slice containing the stone. Take the two external slices and score the flesh in a grid pattern. Push each slice inside out, then using a sharp knife cut the cubes of fruit off the skin. With the central slice, cut off the skin, then trace around the stone and cut it away from the flesh. Put the skinless fruit into a blender, pour over the alcohol and lime juice, and pulse to create a thick, smooth liquid. Try a little, and add sugar to taste. Put the ice into the blender and blend until it is completely amalgamated with the drink.

Pour into four chilled glasses, garnish with cocktail umbrellas and serve.

The Rocky Horror Picture Show

(Jim Sharman, 1975)

The Rocky Horror Picture Show is the cinematic equivalent of Marmite. Most people either love it or hate it, so which side of the divide are you on? I'm not sure myself. The film puts one of the all-time great comic performances on screen (Tim Curry as the gloriously perverse Dr Frank N. Furter) right next to one of the all-time worst (Little Nell as a nasally voiced, screeching hoofer). It offers a wry, affectionate satire on old Hollywood B movies, but is best known for filling cinemas with hairy-legged men bouncing around in ripped stockings and suspenders and throwing rice at each other. While it's still a tale of homosexuality, murder, cannibalism and cross-dressing alien invaders, it's now almost as inoffensively mainstream as *Little House on the Prairie*. And much as I enjoy the musical numbers, if one more person invites me to do the Time Warp again at some rubbish party, they may, like Meatloaf, end up on the menu of my next dinner.

Squeaky-clean Brad Majors (Barry Bostwick) and Janet Weiss (Susan Sarandon) are an earnest young couple so indigestibly wholesome that practically the only thing that could ever shake them out of their all-American innocence is being abducted by a posse of intergalactic trannies. Thank goodness, then, that the winsome pair take a wrong turning on their way to visit Dr Everett Scott (Jonathan Adams) and find themselves with a flat tyre at the gates of a shadowy Gothic pile. For it is there that they are greeted by Riff Raff (Richard O'Brien) and Magenta (Patricia Quinn), gloomy servants of an unnamed master who is about to rock their little world in ways they couldn't imagine.

There, too, they are confronted with the imperiously slinky Dr Frank N. Furter, a delirious cross-dressing mixture of Mick Jagger and *Cabaret*'s Sally Bowles. Despite strutting around half naked with his chest rug bristling under a leather bustier, Frank is actually a brilliant scientist about to realize his ultimate project: the creation of a perfect muscleman to satisfy his every whim. His invention, Rocky (Peter Hinwood), is indeed a vision of muscular perfection in gold lamé pants. But can Dr Frank really control him? As Frank descends into yet more madcapery, butchering former favourite Eddie (Meatloaf) with an ice pick and putting both Brad and Janet out of their virgin misery by seducing them, his control of his strapping creation seems as unsteady as his tottering stilettoed gait.

Poor Eddie, Frank's former golden boy, ends up getting eaten by the cast, so the obvious choice of dish to accompany the film would be meatloaf (see *Rebel Without a Cause*). Still, if you look closely at the movie's dinner scene, the actual dish served up is a piece of roast pork. While many people will rear in horror at the thought of putting pork with Coke, marinating meat in fizzy drinks is quite a common practice in the States, and tenderizes the meat nicely. If you can't find a willing victim to donate the meat for this recipe, remember that pork is supposed to be the closest thing to human flesh (which cannibals call 'long pig') and will do almost as well, especially in this dish, which strikes a nice balance between the trashiness and saucy-spiciness that made the film such a hit.

Roast Long Pig with Coca-Cola Gravy

1 piece pork belly, weighing around 1.5kg (3½ lb)
1 can Coke
juice of 1 lemon
1 teaspoon grated fresh ginger
½ teaspoon cayenne pepper
½ teaspoon paprika

¼ teaspoon allspice
1 teaspoon chopped thyme
2 tablespoons salt
1 onion, chopped
2 cloves garlic, minced
100ml (4 fl oz) vegetable stock
1 teaspoon cornflour (optional)

Plus

a stanley knife, or other very sharp knife

Place the pork in a flat container and cover with the Coke and lemon juice. Cover and leave to marinade overnight, turning at least once. Remove the meat and set the marinade aside, then dry the meat thoroughly with kitchen paper. First, take all the herbs and spices and rub them hard into the meaty underside of the belly. Then take your Stanley knife and cut lots of little grooves across the surface of the fat, at a finger's width from one another (these are necessary to create proper crackling). You need to go about halfway into the fat, without cutting through to the meat. Take the salt and a little extra paprika and rub hard into the fat. Leave this for half an hour, then return and dust off any loose salt.

Place the meat in a roasting tin with the skin face down, and strew this with the onion and garlic. Roast in the top of an oven preheated to 200°C/400°F/Mark 6 for 90 minutes. When the time has elapsed, turn the skin upwards to crisp into proper crackling. At this stage, you can either put your oven on its highest setting or put the meat under the grill, cooking until the skin is all a deep-brown colour.

Leave the meat to rest, while you put the roasting pan on a low heat on top of the stove. Add a quarter of the Coke marinade (discard the rest) and the stock to the pan and bring to the boil, scraping the pan bottom with a wooden spoon to dislodge any juices. Boil this down by half. If you wish to make the gravy a little thicker, sieve in a teaspoonful of cornflour and stir it while it's still boiling until all lumps have completely disintegrated.

Skim the sauce of excess fat, then strain it and serve with slices of the meat, plus roast potatoes or steamed rice.

The Wicker Man

(Robin Hardy, 1973)

With naked couples rutting in graveyards, palm trees flourishing in the highland wastes, schoolgirls worshipping the phallus and spooky Christopher Lee as the local landlord, something fishy is clearly going on in Summerisle.

Prudish Presbyterian sourpuss Sergeant Howie (Edward Woodward) of the West Highland Constabulary smells a rat instantly when he flies to the remote Scottish island searching for a missing girl called Rowan. There he unwittingly stumbles into a neo-pagan version of Royston Vasey, where open fornication is seen as a public duty, the local church is derelict and instead of learning the three Rs, schoolboys gallivant around maypoles singing a whole lot of hippy nonsense (a fairly standard 70s education, then). Not only do the islanders meet Howie's enquiries about Rowan with tight-lipped denial, the pub landlord's daughter Willow (Britt Ekland) even tries to nibble his virgin cherry – but when he keeps his legs crossed, makes do with humping his bedroom door instead. What on earth is going on?

The key lies with the island's owner Lord Summerisle (Christopher Lee). His Victorian philanthropist grandfather, he explains, bought the island and, using new, ultra-hardy strains of tree, turned a barren rock into a fruit grower's paradise. But along with the apples he also brought the old pagan gods back to Summerisle, hoping to put a bit of spunk back into the downtrodden islanders. As the trees started to bear fruit, the locals abandoned the church, going back to the good old ways, curing sore throats with frogs and trying to suck up to the gods by making offerings to them.

But is there a darker side to Summerisle's lusty religion? Sergeant Howie becomes convinced that there may be a connection between Rowan's disappearance and the failure of the previous year's harvest. When his plane is sabotaged, he finds himself stuck on the island as it prepares for its May Day celebrations. As the locals start creeping out of the corners wearing scary masks, can he find Rowan before she gets made into toast for the gods of the harvest?

In these enlightened times, there's no need to sacrifice an entire human to appease the gods – a baked totem will do, as demonstrated by the many candied wicker men in Summerisle's sweet shop. This recipe gives you a chance to burn your own wicker man upon the fire, or maybe just nibble his limbs with your tea. You can also use the recipe to make smaller standard-sized gingerbread men – but if your crops fail, don't hold me responsible.

Whisky and Ginger Wicker Man

60g (2 oz) butter
100g (4 oz) soft brown sugar
150g (5½ oz) treacle
400g (14 oz) self-raising flour
2 teaspoons ground ginger
½ teaspoon ground cinnamon
(optional)

½ teaspoon bicarbonate of soda
½ teaspoon salt
4 or 5 tablespoons whisky
(roughly 40ml)

Plus

greaseproof paper (essential)
woad (optional)

Cream the butter and sugar until fully mixed, then pour in the treacle and beat in with a wooden spoon. Add the flour, spices, soda and salt and carefully blend them into the treacle mixture. Once the treacle is mostly absorbed in the flour, it works best if you use your hands, rubbing the mixture into fine crumbs. Add four tablespoons of the whisky and bring the mixture together, forming it into a large ball. If it is still a little crumbly, add another tablespoonful.

Turn the ball on to a floured surface and split it into two. Roll one part into a ball, and split the remaining part into three smaller portions, so that you now have one large ball and three small ones. The larger ball will be the wicker man's trunk, the three smaller his arms and head. Take the largest ball and roll it into a long cylinder on a large piece of greaseproof paper. Using a rolling pin, flatten this out to the thickness of your little-finger knuckle to make a long round-ended strip. Roll two of the three smaller balls into similar cylinders, then flatten with the rolling pin. For the head, take the remaining piece and flatten into a disc.

Attach the limbs and head to the wicker man's trunk and press firmly to join them. Trim the figure of any ragged edges (any excess dough can be used to make another figure – a wicker rabbit or terrapin, perhaps). Score a groove down the bottom of the man's trunk, but do not cut through to create legs. Using a small, sharp knife, carve the features of your choice upon your man and score a wicker pattern across his body.

Lifting the greaseproof paper on which you have assembled him, put the man on a baking sheet. Place in an oven preheated to 180°C/350°F/Mark 4 and bake for 15 minutes. Remove your clothes, slather yourself with woad (or some similar body paint) and dance joyously in front of the oven as the sacrifice bakes. When he is fully baked, take him out of the oven and leave to cool fully before attempting to remove him from the baking tin (he is very fragile).

A Clockwork Orange

(Stanley Kubrick, 1971)

Young Alex de Large (Malcolm McDowell) is a nasty piece of work with a fondness for spiky eyeliner, assault, battery and Beethoven. Cruising round town with his droogs, he enjoys nothing more than a bit of rape and murder after downing a few jars of Moloko Plus.

His sociopath leanings aren't entirely incomprehensible, though: Alex's world is certainly a strange, twisted place. An ultraviolent day-glo version of 1970s northern England, it's at once gaudily futuristic and curiously old-fashioned, a place where senseless violence is rife and young people speak cod-Russian, but hooligans still live with their parents and hang out in milkbars. While the sets look like discarded backdrops from *Blake's 7*, Alex's mum and dad are neon-wigged versions of Mr Humphries and Mrs Slocombe from *Are You Being Served?*

Alex and his ugly band tear around creating brutal mayhem wherever they go, until one day Alex is finally caught by the police for smashing a woman's Gulliver in with an outsized marble phallus, and thrown into prison. Sentenced to fourteen years, he adapts to the demands of his new surroundings pretty quickly. By brown-nosing the prison chaplain and professing contrition, he soon becomes a model prisoner, though how deep his remorse really goes is a matter for debate.

His lickspittle keenness gets him put forward as a guinea-pig for the Ludovico technique. A short sharp shock of reform so intense that the mere thought of evil-doing will nauseate him in the future, the technique, the government hopes, will eradicate criminality and even subversion. But can you really compel someone to be good by taking away their free will to err? As we see Alex strapped down with his eyes pinned open as part of his treatment, are we witnessing the birth of a new man, or simply the coercion of a flawed human into a docile but amoral clockwork toy?

Alex and his droogs are notoriously hard on anyone overly fond of alcohol, themselves preferring to drink the more swingingly modern alternative, drugged milk. What follows is a version of their favourite tipple, Moloko Drencom. I'm hardly going to recommend anyone puts illegal drugs in their milk (it would taste foul), so in this recipe it's spiked with the formerly banned absinthe, which, though alcoholic, contains thujone, a chemical once thought to drive people mad.

Moloko Drencom

4 teaspoons icing sugar

4 dessertspoons cream

1 litre (35 fl oz) milk

100ml (4 fl oz) absinthe (ideally
Swiss or French, not Czech)

25ml (1 tablespoon) Kahlua
(coffee liqueur)

ice

½ teaspoon cinnamon

Place the sugar in the cream, and stir until fully dissolved. Pour this into the milk, then pour all the ingredients except the cinnamon into an ice-filled cocktail shaker. Shake hard until condensation appears on the outside of the shaker. Pour the drink into four tall glasses and sieve a little dusting of cinnamon on top of each.

Audition

(Takashi Miike, 1999)

With our everyday personas characterized by manipulation and deceit, it's only in moments of extreme agony that we reveal our true selves. At least, that's the opinion of cute little sadist Asami Yamasaki (Eihi Shiina), heroine of director Takashi Miike's notoriously grisly serving of art-house schlock.

Pretty and sweet as a Hello Kitty fridge magnet, Asami stumbles into the life of middle-aged widower Shigeharu Aoyama (Ryo Ishibashi) one day at an audition for a TV film. Asami doesn't yet realize she's been duped: the film is entirely bogus, and lonely TV producer Shigeharu has dreamt up the project as a way to look for a new wife. Unsure how to go about fishing for his ideal woman, a colleague has suggested a shifty, manipulative plan to set up a fake audition where the female lead needs to have all the qualities Shigeharu is looking for in a mate. All he then has to do is take the most suitable applicant out on a date, woo her with expensive food and wine and then make her sign on the dotted line.

The ruse goes perfectly when he meets shy, sweet-tempered Asami. She's a pretty, solitary young woman whose hopes of becoming a ballerina have been ruined by an injury.

With her dreams shattered, now she has nothing in her lonely life except Shigeharu's friendship and her own unhappy childhood memories. Well, that and a one-fingered, footless gimp tied up in a burlap sack. For Asami isn't quite the submissive doll she at first appears. Shigeharu's colleague discovers that all the references on her application were false, and that most places which she claims to frequent have been the sites of spectacularly savage murders. In relation to such an innocuous-looking woman, none of it makes sense, but as the skies around her darken, Shigeharu is just beginning to get an inkling of what he's let himself in for. He might well have felt the need for female companionship, but is he now literally dying for a shag?

This recipe is a traditional Japanese way of preparing the ambiguously gendered sea bream we see Shigeharu catch at the film's outset, and whose ovaries his son so enjoys fiddling with later on. I've chosen to combine it with a sharp, refreshing seaweed salad. Bream grilled in salt is a popular dish to serve at Japanese wedding celebrations (the two lead characters have just become engaged) and at New Year. While there may not seem to be much to it as a recipe, casing the fish in salt keeps the flesh wonderfully moist, and also neutralizes any fishy odours. If sea bream is not available, you could cook any type of mullet or even mackerel this way with great success.

ASIA EXTREME

Salt-grilled Sea Bream with Wakame Salad

4 small or 2 large sea bream
    (the Japanese do not favour
    massive portions), gutted
    and cleaned

roughly 8 tablespoons salt,
    depending on the size of your
    fish
lemon

For the salad

½ cucumber
½ teaspoon salt
20g (¾ oz) dried wakame
    seaweed (see p. 269)
½ white radish

1 tablespoon soy sauce
3 tablespoons rice vinegar
1 teaspoon caster sugar
2 tablespoons roasted sesame
    seeds

For the fish, rub the skin of each one lightly with a little of the salt, then sprinkle both sides of each with a very thick layer of the stuff. The amount you will need varies, but the idea is to create a layer thick enough to form an insulating crust which will later be removed.

Leave the fish for ten minutes so that the salt can harden slightly, then place them carefully under a medium preheated grill for about 7 minutes a side, until properly golden-brown. As you turn the fish over, pour extra salt on any cracks in the casing of the as yet uncooked layer. As they cook, the salt-encrusted skin will shrivel and contract. When the fish are cooked, take a knife and carefully scrape or flick the skin off (you'll find it comes off easily). Take care to remove all the salt. You will now be left with fish whose flesh is still pleasantly moist, despite a hard grilling, and with a perfectly moderate level of saltiness. Put them on a dish and leave your guests to pick away at them with chopsticks.

Serve with lemon wedges and the following wakame salad.

For the salad, cut the cucumber into thin strips and sprinkle with the salt. Leave it in a colander for half an hour while the salt draws out the excess liquid. When the time has elapsed, wipe off the liquid it has sweated, along with the salt, with some kitchen towel. Meanwhile, soak the wakame in hot water for half an hour until completely rehydrated. Drain it and squeeze out the soaking liquid. Peel the radish and cut into thin strips like the cucumber. Gather the wakame into a tight bunch and shred into fine strands with a sharp knife. Mix the soy sauce, vinegar, sugar and sesame seeds together. Combine this with the vegetables and seaweed and toss well to coat.

Leave the flavours to blend for half an hour before serving.

Dark Water

(Hideo Nakata, 2002)

Japanese director Hideo Nakata doesn't need a cannibal psychiatrist or a bloke with a spiky hand to send shivers down your spine – all he needs is a little girl's satchel, a bit of grainy CCTV footage and some dodgy plumbing.

In his *Dark Water*, arguably one of the saddest horror films since *Frankenstein*, we follow the story of recently divorced mother Yoshimi (Hitomi Kuroki) and her five-year-old daughter Ikuko (Rio Kanno) as they look for a new flat. By Japanese standards, the dour, grey block they decide to move into is incredibly old (though by the looks of it, I own socks of a considerably more venerable age). But it's only once the removal men have gone that Yoshimi notices her ageing flat's major flaw, a dripping damp patch on the ceiling of her daughter's bedroom. The building's caretaker shows no interest in fixing the leak, and as Yoshimi is already on the edge of a breakdown due to her custody battle for Ikuko with her ex-husband, she lets the matter drop.

Unfortunately, the unexpected water feature isn't the only strange thing about their new home. When Ikuko finds a schoolbag stuffed with toys on the roof, the caretaker throws it away – so why does it keep reappearing in the same place? And why, when everybody insists the flat upstairs from them is empty, do they keep hearing the patter of little steps in the room above? Meanwhile, Ikuko is starting to act strangely at her new kindergarten, suffering fainting spells and constantly chatting to a friend that no one else can see. As a ghostly figure starts to peek from behind corners and the drip, drip, drip of suspense turns into a flood, it becomes clear that Yoshimi is going to need more than just a plunger and a wrench to staunch the steady flow of creepiness invading her daughter's life.

I've chosen to pair *Dark Water* with shabu shabu, a deliciously fresh way of lightly poaching food at the table that is very popular in Japan. Why? Well, just like the plot of the film, the method involves plunging tender flesh into darkened liquid, and holding it underneath the shimmering surface just until it goes limp – though I wouldn't recommend the method with anything more unorthodox than beef.

Exactly how you serve your shabu shabu depends on what equipment you have at home. Fondue pans work well for keeping the broth warm, as do electric slow cookers. However, the strength of burners under fondue pans varies: while some are hot enough to keep the broth on a gentle simmer, others can be too weak, in which case you will need to cook your food on the hob – or if it's a fine night, you could try it out in the open air on a camping stove.

The ponzu dipping sauce will keep for a week in the fridge and makes a good accompaniment to many Japanese meat dishes, as well as an excellent marinade.

Beef Shabu Shabu with Ponzu Dipping Sauce

1 litre (35 fl oz) water
30g (1 oz) strip kombu
   (see p. 267)
5 dried shiitake mushrooms
6 carrots
1 leek

1 Japanese or Chinese cabbage
400g (14 oz) beef fillet
10 fresh shiitake mushrooms
1 clump fresh enokitake
   mushrooms (optional; see
   p. 266)

For the ponzu dipping sauce

200ml (7 fl oz) mirin (see p. 268)
120ml (4½ fl oz) rice vinegar
4 tablespoons soy sauce
30g (1 oz) katsuobushi (dried
   bonito flakes; see p. 266)

juice of 4 limes (or, if you can
   find it, Yuzu – a Japanese
   citrus fruit occasionally found
   fresh in Eastern Asian stores)
zest of 1 lime

Heat the water in a saucepan until hot, but not boiling, and throw in the kombu and the shiitake mushrooms. Turn off the heat. Cover the pan and leave the contents to infuse for a couple of hours, then light a flame under the pan again and heat the liquid very gently. Heat it yet again to very close to boiling, then strain off the kombu and mushrooms. You now have the broth you're going to use to cook your shabu shabu.

Just before you are ready to eat, peel the carrots, trim the leek and cabbage and along with the fresh mushrooms cut them all into bite-sized chunks. Cut your beef fillet into very thin slices with a sharp knife and put on a serving dish. Heat the broth to a low simmer – and transfer to your heated fondue pan if you are using one. Throw a few chunks of vegetable into the broth and leave to cook for about 5 minutes. Meanwhile, take slices of the beef and throw them into the simmering broth with chopsticks. Remove the beef when it is just cooked – 10 seconds is often enough for very thin slices – and eat dipped in the ponzu sauce. As the vegetables cook, throw more chunks in to replace the ones you eat.

To make the ponzu, mix all of the ingredients except the lime juice in a saucepan and bring slowly to the boil. Remove from the heat once it has boiled, strain the liquid and add the lime juice.

Battle Royale

(Kinji Fukasaku, 2000)

The Japanese know a thing or two about proper discipline. When Class B of Shiroiwa Junior High School start bunking off lessons, they don't just get a stiff talking-to and a letter home, as they would in soft-touch Britain. Oh no – they're taken away on a school field trip, gassed asleep, and then woken up once they have had metal collars fitted that will blow their heads up if they so much as whisper out of turn.

These may already seem like strong measures, especially for a class that can make the effort to come on a school trip in immaculately correct school uniform. But this is only the beginning, for *Battle Royale* takes place in a nightmarish imaginary version of modern Japan, where 10 million are unemployed and the Establishment are so afraid of young delinquents that the best idea they have for controlling them is to make them take part in a gory real-life video game.

Class B's captor turns out to be their bitter old teacher Mr Kitano (Beat Takeshi), who left the school in despair after failing to reform them. But whereas once he couldn't even prevent himself from being stabbed by unruly pupils, he now thinks nothing of knifing one through the head, just for whispering while he's talking. Mr Kitano tells Class B what is about to become of them. Transported to a deserted island, the class have three days in which to kill each other, or themselves be exterminated. If they refuse to do so, every single one will be blown up by their irremovable collars. Each student is provided with a bag of provisions and a weapon.

While the lucky ones get machine-guns perfect for mowing down the competition, others have to make do with woefully undeadly tools such as a not particularly large saucepan lid, which could only be useful for decapitating someone if you had patience, an exceptionally strong arm and a heavily sedated victim. Many of the pupils swear they won't be lured into butchering their classmates, but with a few unwelcome jokers in the pack running amok from minute one, and the fear of ending up as sashimi taking its toll, the beautifully green island they've been dumped on quickly starts turning red.

Given the impressionable, difficult age of most of *Battle Royale*'s characters, it's only fitting to accompany the film with a recipe for something Japanese teenagers are known to enjoy.

Originating in Taiwan in the 90s, bubble tea is now hugely popular with young people all over East Asia, with specialist tea parlours selling the drink and little else. Closer to a milkshake than a conventional tea, it usually consists of cold sweet tea flavoured with fruit pulp or syrup and served up with a bottom layer of jelly-like tapioca pearls, which you can suck up your straw and chew as you drink. The more sober of palate might find this intensely fruity recipe rather sweet – but as they have no more than three days to live, the teenagers of *Battle Royale* are hardly inclined to worry about their teeth rotting prematurely.

Bubble Royale Fruity Pearl Tea

water
3 tablespoons tapioca pearls
   (see p. 269)
100g (4 oz) granulated sugar
500ml (17 fl oz) weak Japanese
   green tea
300g (10½ oz) raspberries
200ml (7 fl oz) pineapple juice
   (you can also use passion

fruit, cranberry or apple,
   as long as it isn't too sharp –
   citrus juices are too acid and
   may curdle the milk)
40–50g (1½–2 oz) (3 or 4
   tablespoons) condensed milk,
   depending on how sweet your
   tooth is
ice cubes

Plus

extra-wide straws

Bring a litre (35 fl oz) of water to the boil in a large saucepan. Add the tapioca pearls and return to the boil, stirring them every five minutes or so. Cook until the pearls have become jelly-like, with only a small amount of white still visible in their otherwise translucent centres. This normally takes about 45 minutes. To test whether they are finished or not, fish a pearl out of the saucepan with a spoon, let it cool slightly, then chew it. Is its centre very close to soft? Then it's ready. Bear in mind that the pearls will continue to soften after they have been removed from the heat, so a tiny bit of resistance is not necessarily a problem.

While the pearls are boiling, heat another 120ml (4½ fl oz) of water in another saucepan. Add the sugar, stir until it dissolves and then bring the syrup to the boil. Remove from the heat and leave covered to keep warm. When the pearls are ready, return the syrup to almost boiling, then take it off the heat. Drain the pearls from their cooking liquid, then stir them into the syrup. Leave them to soak in the syrup for 30 minutes.

Meanwhile, make the green tea. You don't want it very strong, so pour it out after a couple of minutes' brewing into a jug or bowl where it can cool quickly. Press the raspberries through a sieve to remove the pulp, then discard the seeds. Once the pearls have finished soaking in the syrup, pour in the tea. When the tea and syrup blend is cool, add the raspberry pulp and pineapple juice and stir well. Put the condensed milk in a bowl and very slowly add dribbles of the tea-syrup to it, stirring it constantly to blend the two together – if you add the tea too fast, there is a danger that the milk will curdle. When you have stirred enough in to make a very thin liquid, pour it back into the rest of the tea and stir to blend. Leave this mixture in the fridge to chill fully.

When it is cold, divide the tea between 4 very large glasses (pint glasses are a good size), and ladle a helping of pearls into each one. Add a few ice cubes to each glass and serve with straws wide enough to suck up the pearls with.

BONUS FEATURES

Unusual Foods and Where to Find Them

I've tried to give a useful, comprehensive list of the more difficult-to-find ingredients from the book – with brief explanations and, where possible, suggestions of where they can be bought.

ABSINTHE: A strong, aniseed-flavoured spirit which was once banned in many countries, due to the use of the aromatic herb wormwood in its production. In the nineteenth century, it was believed that the presence of the chemical thujone in wormwood could lead absinthe drinkers to suffer hallucinations and epilepsy. Despite the best efforts of absinthe manufacturers keen to sell their product as psychoactive rocket fuel, this view has now been entirely discredited, and the drink contains only a very small amount of the chemical anyway. The 90s saw an absinthe revival in Britain, with Czech-produced brands, such as Hill's, leading the market. Unfortunately, while Czech brands all contain wormwood, they often contain little or none of the fennel and anise that give the spirit much of its characteristic flavour, so you're really better off with a French or Swiss brand (Switzerland was the country where the spirit was first produced). Absinthe is now on sale in many larger off-licences, but if you have trouble getting hold of some, or can only find Bohemian-style brands, you can order authentic versions of the drink online. Some reliable websites among many are www.eabsinthe.com, www.absintheclassics.com and www.beersofeurope.com.

ADUKI BEANS: These small red beans are popular throughout China, Korea and Japan. They are typically eaten sweetened, and often made into pastes. As well as being available here in Japanese or Chinese shops, they are quite common in health food stores nowadays as well.

ADVOCAAT: A thick, creamy liqueur made with eggs, sugar and brandy, advocaat is fairly easy to get hold of and on sale in most larger off-licences. As well as being a cocktail ingredient, it's rather nice poured over ice-cream as a sauce. If you're visiting Germany and enjoy advocaat, it's worth seeking out the chocolate cups that supermarkets sell around Christmastime, so you can eat your glass once you've drunk its contents.

ASAFOETIDA: Despite going under the unappetizing name of 'devil's dung', asafoetida is actually a subtle and interesting spice. Its use in this book is as a stand-in for *silphium*, the most prized spice in the Classical world, with which it is believed to be identical. Though the plant whose sap is used to make the condiment had probably died out in Europe by the Dark Ages, it is still widely used in India, and any shop selling a reasonable range of Indian spices should have it on sale.

ASIAN FIVE SPICE: A Chinese spice blend normally containing cinnamon, cassia buds, star anise, ginger root and ground cloves. The blend is easy to get hold of in most supermarkets (Schwartz produce a version).

BUCKWHEAT: Used to make Japanese noodles (also known as soba noodles), which are are less common and more expensive than standard wheatflour noodles, but have a distinctive nutty flavour that makes them worth the extra cash.

Though they are treated as cereals, buckwheat groats are actually the seeds of a bush. With an ability to grow in cold climates, buckwheat is widely eaten in Poland and Russia (as *kasha*), and its flour is used to make savoury crêpes (or *galettes*) in Brittany. Buckwheat noodles are generally made with a combination of buckwheat and wheat flour, and are often eaten cold in salads. As they are lower in gluten than standard wheat noodles, soba are now commonly available in most health food shops, as well as at Japanese and Korean groceries.

CHILLIES, ANCHO AND GUAJILLO: The intense heat of jalapeño and habanero peppers makes most people understandably wary of cooking with chillies. However, many of the commonest Mexican peppers are actually only medium-hot. Both anchos and guajillos are relatively mild: anchos have a slightly sweet, raisiny flavour, while guajillos are tangier, with undertones of tomato. Both chillies normally come smoke-dried, which gives them an extra taste layer that is intensely savoury and quite delicious. As well as being used in the recipe in this book, these chillies work well ground in a mortar, then diluted into a thin sauce with corn or olive oil. This makes an excellent condiment for tacos, or even guacamole. You can buy both varieties online at www.coolchile.co.uk or www.thespiceshop.co.uk. The latter has a shop, at 1 Blenheim Crescent, London W11 2EE (tel: 0207 221 4448), which has an excellent selection of just about every spice you could want.

CRUMPET RINGS: Designed to keep crumpets in shape during their first toasting, these rings aren't easy to get hold of. They can be bought online, however, at Amazon.com – that is, the American site, not the British one – where they are on sale for $3.95 as

'English muffin rings'. Alternatively, use high-sided metal biscuit-cutters or egg rings, very well greased.

ENOKITAKE MUSHROOMS: These delicate Japanese mushrooms come bunched together in tiny white strands, looking like clusters of squid tentacles. They are occasionally to be found in larger supermarkets, alongside the far more common shiitake. They are not essential for any recipe in this book, but make a pleasingly unusual ingredient for shabu shabu.

FRANGELICO: A deliciously nutty Italian liqueur made by macerating hazelnuts and herbs in spirit, then straining and sweetening the resulting liquid. It's rather sweet on its own, but goes well mixed with espresso as an after-dinner digestif, or, mixed with lemonade or soda water and a twist of lime, as a refreshing summer cocktail. It's not the most common of liqueurs and is usually only available at more specialist wine merchants. It can, though, easily be found online (along with many other spirits) at www.beersofeurope.co.uk.

KABANOS: A dried, smoked Polish pork sausage, long and thin, and that is often flavoured with caraway seed. As you would expect, the sausage has a fairly dry, dense texture. Normally eaten without any extra cooking, it makes an excellent snack with gherkins and a glass of frozen flavoured vodka. Due to recent Polish migration, kabanos are now available even in relatively remote parts of the country, wherever there are shops catering to Poles. The sausages are also sold by a few supermarkets, notably Budgens, which has an especially good range of Polish products.

KATSUOBUSHI: The dried fermented and smoked flakes of the flesh of skipjack tuna, otherwise known as bonito. The flakes are always bought prepacked nowadays, and are a basic building-block of dashi broth, one of the most common ingredients of Japanese cooking. Any shop catering to Japanese customers will sell these, but if you don't have one nearby, you can buy them online at www.japancentre.com (posted from Britain) or www.jp-stores.com (shipped from Japan).

KIRSCHWASSER: The name of this German spirit means 'cherry water', and it's an eau de vie distilled from the juice of fermented black cherries. As well as making a fine after-dinner tipple, it is also widely used in cooking, most notably in dishes such as fondue and Black Forest gateau. Kirschwasser is mainly confined to specialist wine merchants in this country, but due to the overlap between German traditions and those of the French province of Alsace, it can be found on sale in the fairly large French wine chain Nicolas. For online stockists try www.the drinkshop.com or www.beersofeurope.co.uk.

KOMBU: This sea vegetable is a member of the kelp family. Its most common use is as a basis for the dashi broth so ubiquitous in Japanese cuisine. Beyond shops catering to Japanese customers, kombu can also be bought in many health food stores. For online suppliers, see those listed at *katsuobushi* above.

LILLET BLANC: A white vermouth made in south-western France, Lillet Blanc is perhaps most famous nowadays on account of Bond's mention of the drink, as Kina Lillet, in *Casino Royale*. He was in fact rather out of date, as by the time the book was published, 'Kina' had been dropped from the brand name. Lillet Blanc differs from other vermouths in its relatively high quinine content (the stuff that gives tonic water its taste), though this was substantially reduced in 1985, simply because no one seemed to like it. Again, this is rather a specialist brand, but is available online at www.thedrinkshop.com.

LUMPFISH CAVIAR: The roe of the ugly-faced lumpsucker or lumpfish, very popular in Scandinavia, and a good stand-in when you want something that might possibly be mistaken for real sturgeon caviar (hardly anyone's tried the real thing anyway). It's available in larger supermarkets, many delicatessens, and at IKEA.

MIRIN: A slightly sweet Japanese rice wine, lower in alcohol than sake, and which is often used in cooking. Mirin is sold by the standard Japanese suppliers mentioned at *katsuobushi* above.

MUFFIN CASES, HIGH-SIDED: Slightly larger than the standard paper cake cups most often found in British supermarkets. Many shops now stock them, but if you can only find fairy-cake cups, you can buy jumbo muffin cases online at www.cakecraft shop.co.uk.

OCTOPUS, BABY: Baby octopus isn't that easy to get hold of fresh. East Asian supermarkets often sell them frozen, however, and if you don't have one of these nearby, your regular fishmonger should be able to order you a bag.

ROSEWATER: This delicately scented liquid is extremely popular as a flavouring for sweet dishes in India, the Middle East and the eastern Mediterranean, and is a by-product of the process of distilling the rose oil used in perfumes. As well as being used in confectionery, it adds an interesting flavour to any syrup for poaching fruit. Many supermarkets stock it in the baking section and it can also be bought in many Indian, Middle Eastern and

Greek grocers. If you can't find it, it can be bought online at www.natco-online.com.

SMOKED PORK LOIN: A smoky, brined and relatively lean pork product popular throughout Central and Eastern Europe. In Germany, where the originally Russian recipe using it in this book (*solyanka*) comes from, it is called *Kassler*. In this country, you are more likely to find it in shops selling Polish food, where it is called *poledwica* (pronounced po-lend-*weet*-sa). If you have a Greek or Cypriot shop nearby they may also stock it, under the name *loundza*. It's also often available in the recently spread Polish sections of many supermarket chains. It's generally better if you buy it in a single block, rather than sliced, and cut it into dice yourself. If you can't get hold of it, you could use some boiled gammon, though the flavour is rather different.

TAPIOCA PEARLS: White balls made of starch from the cassava plant, originally from South America. When fully cooked, they swell and turn transparent. Once popular as a cheap carbohydrate for puddings, tapioca pearls have no real taste of their own and have fallen out of fashion in the West. They are still popular in Brazil, however, as well as in East Asia, where they are much liked for their dense jelly-like bounce on the tongue, and as the chewy component of bubble teas. You can buy tapioca pearls in any shop stocking Chinese or Thai food, and many Japanese shops as well.

WAKAME: This extremely tenacious edible seaweed has now spread from its East Asian homeland across the world, and can be found growing on British coasts. It has thin, delicate fronds and is usually added to soups or salads. Like all edible seaweeds, it is exceptionally nutritious and high in minerals – for this reason it is now available in many health food stores as well as in Japanese shops. For websites selling dried wakame, see *katsuobushi* above.

WONTON WRAPPERS: Making the thin pasta-like wrappers necessary for wonton is quite a fiddly process, but they can be bought frozen in East Asian food shops, where a standard pack contains about fifty. This may sound like a lot, but bear in mind that each wrapper will hold only a teaspoonful of stuffing.

Recommended Chinese, Japanese and East Asian Food Stores

Fuji Food Stores
The Shopping Forum
18–22 Jesus Lane
Cambridge CB5 8QB
Tel: 01223 308008

Japan Centre
212 Piccadilly
London W1J 9HG
Tel: 020 7255 8255

Loon Fung Supermarket
42–44 Gerrard Street
London W1D 5QG
Tel: 020 7437 7332

Okinami
12 York Place
Brighton BN1 4GU
Tel: 01273 677702

See Woo
The Point
29 Saracen Street
Hamilton Hill
Glasgow G22 5HT
Tel: 0845 078 8818

Wing Yip
375 Nechells Park Road
Nechells
Birmingham B7 5NT
Tel: 0121 327 3838

also at:
395 Edgware Road
London NW2 6LN
Tel: 020 8450 0422

and at:
Oldham Road
Ancoats
Manchester M4 5HU
Tel: 0161 832 3215

The Pulp Kitchen Movie Collection

As a film-loving gourmand you will no doubt have your own favourite food-related movies, but there may be some you have missed. See below for our list of the all-time cinema classics for the kitchen:

The Texas Chainsaw Moussaka • Withnail and Pie • Scone With The Wind (*the Bollywood version of this*, Gone With the Vinda-loo, *went down the pan*) • The Lamb Shank Redemption • Eggs, Fries and Videotape • Braisers of the Lost Pork • Fry Hard • Apocalypse Chow • The Wild Brunch • A Sweetcar Named Dessert • Bap to the Future • The Big Eat • Gentlemen Prefer Blancmange • Who Strained Roger Rabbit? • Casino Royale with Cheese • On Her Majesty's Silver Service • Fritter from an Unknown Salmon • The Man with the Golden Bun • From Rasher with Love • Planet of the Grapes • The Evil Bread • The Fridges of Madison County • The Sandwiches of Eastwick • A Sausage to India • Quorn Free • Wok the Loin • Curry on up the Khyber or any in the series of 'Curry on' films • Five Easy Pizzas • It's a Wonderful Loaf • American Brewed-tea • Fight Club Sandwich • The Guns of Provolone • Escalope to Victory • The Great Escalope • For Your Pies Only • All Quiet on the Western Sponge • Oyster and Lucinda • Natural Born Grillers • Quiche Largo • Full Metal Jacket Potato • What's Gilbert Grape Eating? • Bring Me the Bread of Alfredo Garcia • Yankee Doodle Candy

PULP KITCHEN

• The Flan Who Wasn't There • The Running Ham • Gangs of New Pork • My Darling Clementine • Sunset Bouillabaise • The Sound of Muesli • Black Forest Gump • Live and Let Fry • Some Bake it Hot (*released in the UK as* Some Like it Hotpot) • Crouching Tiger, Hidden Dragon, Toad in the Hole • Citizen Cake • To Grill a Mockingbird • The Pud, the Flan and the Bubbly • The Cook, the Thief, His Wife and Their Liver (*also* The Cook, the Chef, His Pie and Her Oven, *porn version*) • The Codfather • Reservoir Hotdogs • White Meat • Silence of the Clams • Tarragon in 60 Seconds • The Ploughman's Contract • Whisky Business • Supperman • Donnie Tobasco • Cous Cous, Bang Bang • The Madras of King George • Okrahoma • Yeast of Eden • Rice Age • The Lord of the Onion Rings • Captain Corelli's Mandarin • Gristle Down the Wind • The Inedibles • M*A*S*H • Bedknobs and Drumsticks • Bridget Scones's Diary • The Manchurian Candied Date • Jus et Gin • Dansak With Wolves • Grill Bill • Peel Harbour • The Englishman Who Cooked Up a Krill But Gulped Down a Plantaine • Gosford Pork • Collander Girls • Something's Gotta Sieve

Further Reading

Anger, Kenneth: *Hollywood Babylon*, Bantam Doubleday Dell, 1983

Beeton, Isabella (with Kathryn Hughes): *Mrs. Beeton's Book of Household Management*, Cassell, 2001 (originally published 1861)

Biskind, Peter: *Easy Riders, Raging Bulls: How the Sex 'n' Drugs 'n' Rock 'n' Roll Generation Saved Hollywood*, Bloomsbury, 1999

Bordwell, David and Thompson, Kristin: *Film Art: An Introduction*, McGraw Hill, 2005

Brillat-Savarin, Jean Anthelme: *The Physiology of Taste*, Penguin, 1994 (originally published 1826)

Burchill, Julie: *Girls on Film*, Virgin Books, 1986

Clark, Samantha and Samuel: *Moro: The Cookbook*, Ebury Press, 2001

David, Elizabeth: *French Provincial Cooking*, Penguin, 1987

Davidson, Alan: *The Penguin Companion to Food*, Penguin, 1999

Grigson, Jane: *English Food*, Penguin, 1998

Grigson, Sophie: *The First-Time Cook*, Collins, 2004

Hazan, Marcella: *The Essentials of Classical Italian Cooking*, Macmillan, 1995

Halliwell, Leslie and Walker, John: *Halliwell's Film, Video and DVD Guide*, HarperCollins, 2006

Hopkinson, Simon and Bareham, Lindsay: *The Prawn Cocktail Years*, Macmillan, 1997

Kael, Pauline: *Movie Love: Complete Reviews 1988–1991*, Plume, 1991

Kurihara, Harumi: *Harumi's Japanese Cooking*, Conran Octopus, 2006

Lane, Anthony: *Nobody's Perfect: Writings From the New Yorker*, Picador, 2002

Norrington-Davies, Tom: *Cupboard Love: How to Get the Most Out of Your Kitchen*, Hodder and Stoughton, 2005

Ortiz, Elisabeth Lambert: *Mexican (World Cookery)*, Lorenz, 2004

Roden, Claudia: *The New Book of Middle Eastern Food*, Alfred A. Knopf, 2000

Thomson, David: *The New Biographical Dictionary of Film*, Little, Brown, 2003

Time Out Film Guide 2008, Time Out Guides Ltd, 2007

Waters, Alice and Curtan, Patricia: *Chez Panisse Vegetables*, HarperCollins, 1996

Weiser, Thomas: *Asian Cult Cinema*, Boulevard Books, 2002

Yan-kit, So: *Yan-kit's Classic Chinese Cookbook*, Dorling Kindersley, 1998

Index

300 (2006) 183–5

absinthe
  Moloko Drencom 245
  sourcing 263
Adams, Jonathan 236
Adamson, Andrew 30, 214
Adobo Marinated Trout with Corn
    Salsa 198–9
aduki beans
  Japanese Rice and Bean Cakes
      (Daifuku) 219–20
  sourcing 264
*Adventures of Priscilla, Queen of the
    Desert, The* (1994) 230–1
advocaat
  Dutch Breakfast at Tiffany's 142
  sourcing 264
alcoholic drinks
  Arctic Martini Granita 66
  California Dreamin' Cocktail 208
  Dutch Breakfast at Tiffany's 142
  Mango Daiquiris 232
  Moloko Drencom 245
  Spiced Shire Ale 23
  Vesper Lynd Martini 53
  Wire-cutter Cocktail 229
Ale, Spiced Shire 23
Alien (1979) 113–14

Allen, Corey 133
Allen, Woody 42
Almodovar, Pedro 173
almonds 123–4
Altman, Robert 196
Amélie (2001) 45, 161–2
American indie 191–208
ancho
  Adobo Marinated Trout with
      Corn Salsa 198–9
  sourcing 265
Ancient Roman Barley Stew 181–1
Anderson, Paul Thomas 206
Andress, Ursula 51, 57
Andrews, Julie 72
animation 209–220
Annie Hall (1977) xiv, 42–3
apples
  Cranberry and Apple Pie 204–5
  Liquorice Toffee Apples 212–13
Archer, Anne 197
Arctic Martini Granita 66
asafoetida 264
Asia Extreme 247–60
Asian five spice 264
Asio-Caribbean Papaya Steak
    59–60
Atholl Brose 189–90
Audition (1999) 249–50

INDEX

Bach, Barbara 61
bacon, Pork Loin with Prunes and
    Caraway 171–2
Baker, Kenny 118
Banderas, Antonio 174
Barley Stew, Ancient Roman 181–2
Barranco, María 173
Barrymore, Drew 91
Bates, Kathy xiii
Battle Royale (2000) 257–9
beans
    aduki 219, 264
    Elk and Bean Stew 225–6
    haricot 225–6
    Japanese Rice and Bean Cakes
        (Daifuku) 219–20
    Liver with Fava Beans and Chianti
        85–6
Becker, Wolfgang 157
beef
    Asio-Caribbean Papaya Steak
        59–60
    Beef Shabu Shabu with Ponzu
        Dipping Sauce 255–6
    Clemenza's Sicilian Meatballs 5–6
    Gourmet Doggie Chow 150
    Rebel Meatloaf 134–6
    Steak Tartare 195
Bergman, Ingrid 127
Berkley, Elizabeth xii, 148
Berry, Halle 151
Beurre Blanc, Steamed Lobsters with
    43–4
Bianchi, Daniela 54
Billington, Stephen 188
biscuits, Whisky and Ginger Wicker
    Man 241–2
Black Forest Ice-cream Soda 79–80
Blackmer, Sidney 88
Blair, Linda 93

Bloody Popcorn 92
Blue Soup 47–8
Blue Velvet (1986) 200–1
blueberries
    Blueberry Velvet 201–2
    Cinnamon Crusted Blueberry
        Muffins 12–13
Bogart, Humphrey xiii, 127
Bond films xiv, 49–66
Boogie Nights (1997) 206–7
Bostwick, Barry 235
Bound (1996) 227–8
Boyd, Billy 27
Brando, Marlon 3
brandy
    Fruit Gruel 70–1
    Spiced Shire Ale 23
Braveheart (1995) 187–9
bread
    Lembas Bread 29
    Loaves and Fishes 101–2
    see also Saucy Crumpet
Breakfast at Tiffany's (1961) 140–1
Bresslaw, Bernard 107
Bridget Jones's Diary (2001) 45–6
Brokeback Mountain (2005) 223–4
Brosnan, Pierce 65
Brown, Joe E. 138
Bruhl, Daniel 157
Bubble Royale Fruity Pearl Tea
    259–60
buckwheat
    Lembas Bread 29
    Rebel Meatloaf 134–6
    sourcing 264–5
Burstyn, Ellen 93
Buscemi, Steve 193
Butler, Gerard 183
Buttermilk Fried Chicken 131–2
Butterworth, Peter 107

INDEX

Caan, James xiii, 4

cakes
    Chocolate Orange Angel-food
        Cake 76–7
    Cinnamon Crusted Blueberry
        Muffins 12–13

California Dreamin' Cocktail 208

Campari, Wire-cutter Cocktail 229

Campbell, Martin 51, 64

Campbell, Neve 91

caramel, Cuban Gold Bar (Tocino de
    Cielo) 16–17

caraway
    Caraway and Horseradish
        Coleslaw 41
    Pork Loin with Caraway and
        Prunes 171–2

Carey, Mariah 46

Carry on Camping (1969) xiv,
    107–8

Casablanca (1942) 127–8

Casablancan Fish Soup 129

Casino (1995) 10–11

Casino Royale (2006) 51–3, 267

Cassavetes, John 87

Castellano, Richard 3

Catwoman (2004) 151–2

Caviare, Lumpfish
    Devilled Eggs with 114–16
    sourcing 268

Chadwick, June 104

Chalky Mint Chocolate Mousse 89

champagne, California Dreamin'
    Cocktail 208

Channing, Stockard 78

Chaplin, Charlie 42

Chapman, Graham 99

Char-grilled Baby Octopus 147

cheese dishes, Chicory and Ham
    Gratin 163–4

Cheung, Maggie 165

Chianti, Liver with Fava Beans and
    85–6

Chicken, Buttermilk Fried 131–2

Chicory and Ham Gratin 163–4

chillies
    Adobo Marinated Trout with
        Corn Salsa 198–9
    sourcing 265

Chiu-wai, Tony Leung 165

Chocolat (2000) xv

chocolate
    Black Forest Ice-cream Soda
        79–80
    Chalky Mint Chocolate Mousse
        89
    Chocolate Orange Angel-food
        Cake 76–7

Chronicles of Narnia 30–1

Cinnamon Crusted Blueberry
    Muffins 12–13

Clemenza's Sicilian Meatballs 5–6

Clockwork Orange, A (1971) 243–4

Coca-Cola Gravy, Roast Long Pig
    with 237–8

cocktails
    Arctic Martini Granita 66
    California Dreamin' Cocktail 208
    Dutch Breakfast at Tiffany's 142
    Mango Daiquiris 232
    Moloko Drencom 245
    Vesper Lynd Martini 53
    Wire-cutter Cocktail 229

coconut
    Coconut Frogspawn 216
    Pistachio and Coconut Turkish
        Delight 31–2

Cole, Nat King 166

Coleslaw, Caraway and Horseradish
    41

INDEX

comedy 97–110
Connery, Sean 54, 57
Coppola, Francis Ford 3
Corn Salsa, Adobo Marinated Trout
    with 198–9
Cotten, Joseph 122
Craig, Andrew 51
Cranberry and Apple Pie 204–5
Craven, Wes 90
cream
    Cream Posset 153
    Frozen Raspberry Tits 138–9
crème de menthe 89
Crowe, Russell 179
Crumpet, Saucy 109–10
crumpet rings 265–6
Crystal, Billy 39
Cuban Gold Bar (Tocino de Cielo)
    16–17
cucumber, Gazpacho 175–6
cult films 233–45
Cumberland Sauce, Roast Gammon
    Sandwiches with 105–6
Cumming, Alan 65
Curry, Tim 235
Curtis, Tony 137
Curtiz, Michael 127

da Silva Pereira, José 140–1
Daifuku (Japanese Rice and Bean
    Cakes) 219–20
Daiquiris, Mango 232
Daniels, Anthony 117
Dark Water (2002) 253–4
Day, Doris 174
De Niro, Robert xiii, 7, 10
De Palma, Brian 14
Dean, James 133
Demme, Jonathan 83
Dern, Laura 201

desserts
    Blueberry Velvet 201–2
    Chalky Mint Chocolate Mousse 89
    Chocolate Orange Angel-food
        Cake 76–7
    Cinnamon Crusted Blueberry
        Muffins 12–13
    Coconut Frogspawn 216
    Cranberry and Apple Pie 204–5
    Cream Posset 153
    Cuban Gold Bar (Tocino de Cielo)
        16–17
    Frozen Raspberry Tits 138–9
    Fruit Gruel 70–1
    Gin- and Lime-flavoured Demon
        Bile 95
    Pumpkin Pasties 34–5
    Solyent Green Halva Macaroon
        Squares 123–4
    see also sweets
Devilled Eggs with Lumpfish Caviare
    114–16
Diaz, Cameron 214
Dillon, Matt 203
Disney, Walt 211, 214
Doe Schnitzels 73–4
Donen, Stanley 75
Dover Sole in White Wine 55–6
Dr No (1962) 51, 57–9
drinks
    Black Forest Ice-cream Soda
        79–80
    Bubble Royale Fruity Pearl Tea
        259–60
    see also alcoholic drinks
Dutch Breakfast at Tiffany's 142

Eat Drink Man Woman (1994) xiii
Edwards, Blake 140
eggs

INDEX

Cuban Gold Bar (Tocino de Cielo) 16–17
Devilled Eggs with Lumpfish Caviare 114–16
Ekland, Britt 239
Elk and Bean Stew 225–6
Elliott, Stephen 230
enokitake mushrooms
Beef Shabu Shabu with Ponzu Dipping Sauce 255–6
sourcing 268
Enya 27
Exorcist, The (1973) 93–4

fantasy movies 19–35
Farrow, Mia 87
Fava Beans and Chianti, Liver with 85–6
Fellowship of the Ring, The (2001) 21
Fiennes, Ralph 34
Firth, Colin 46
fish
Adobo Marinated Trout with Corn Salsa 198–9
Casablancan Fish Soup 129
katsuobush 266–7
Loaves and Fishes 101–2
Salt-grilled Sea Bream with Wakame Salad 251–2
Sardinian Mullet Escabeche 63
Sole in White Wine 55–6
Fisher, Carrie 117
Fleischer, Richard 121
foie gras, Gourmet Doggie Chow 150
foreign language films 155–76
Foster, Jodie 83
frangelico
Dutch Breakfast at Tiffany's 142

sourcing 266
From Russia with Love (1963) 54–5
Frozen Raspberry Tits 138–9
Fruit Gruel 70–1
Fukasaku, Kinji 257

Gable, Clark 130
Gammon Sandwiches, Roast, with Cumberland Sauce 105–6
gangster movies xi, 1–17
gay and lesbian films 221–32
Gazpacho 175–6
Gershon, Gina 148, 227
Giannini, Adriano 145
Gibson, Mel 187
Gilbert, Lewis 61
gin
Dutch Breakfast at Tiffany's 142
Gin- and Lime-flavoured Demon Bile 95
Vesper Lynd Martini 53
Ginger and Whisky Wicker Man 241–2
Gladiator (2000) 179–81
Godfather, The (1972) xi, 3–4
GoldenEye (1995) 64–5
Gone with the Wind (1939) 130–1
Goodbye Lenin! (2003) 157–8
Goodfellas (1990) 7–8, 11
Gordon, Ruth 87
Gourmet Doggie Chow 150
Graham, Heather 206
Grant, Cary 138
Grant, Hugh 45
Gratin, Chicory and Ham 163–4
Gravy, Coca-Cola, Roast Long Pig with 237–8
Grease (1978) 78–9
Green, Eva 52
green tea 259–60

INDEX

Gremolata, Razored Garlic, Osso
    Buco with 8–9
grey mullet, Sardinian Mullet
    Escabeche 63
Grint, Rupert 33
guajillo
  Adobo Marinated Trout with
      Corn Salsa 198–9
  sourcing 265
Guest, Christopher 103, 104
Guillén, Fernando 173
Guinness, Alec 118
Gyllenhaal, Jake 223

Hagen, Jean 75
Halva Macaroon Squares, Soylent
    Green 123–4
Ham and Chicory Gratin 163–4
Hamill, Mark 118
Hanly, Peter 188
Hardy, Robin 239
haricot beans, Elk and Bean Stew
    225–6
Harris, Richard 179
Harry Potter and the Goblet of Fire
    (2005) 33–4
Headey, Lena 183
Heald, Anthony 83
Hemingway, Ernest 10
Hendra, Tony 103
Henreid, Paul 128
Hepburn, Audrey 140, 180
Heston, Charlton 122
Hill, Bernard 24
Hinwood, Peter 236
historical epics 177–90
Hollywood gold 125–42
Holm, Ian 21, 114
Hopkins, Anthony 83
Hopper, Dennis 200

horror xiii, 81–95
Horseradish and Caraway Coleslaw
    41
Howard, Leslie 130
Hurt, John 114

Ianevski, Stanislav 33
Ice-cream Soda, Black Forest 79–80
Il Postino (1994) xiii
In the Mood for Love (2000) 165–6
indie films 191–208
Ishibashi, Ryo 249

Jackson, Peter 21, 24, 27
Jacques, Hattie 108
Jagger, Mick 236
James, Sid 107
Janssen, Famke 64
Japanese Rice and Bean Cakes
    (Daifuku) 219–20
Jenson, Vicky 214
Jeunet, Jean-Pierre 161
John, Gottfried 64
Jones, Terry 99
Jones-Davies, Sue 100
Jurgens, Curt 61

kabanos sausages
  Solyanka Soup 159–60
  sourcing 266
Kahlua, Moloko Drencom 245
Kanno, Rio 253
Kar-wai, Wong 165
Kassler 269
Kassovitz, Mathieu 162
katsuobushi
  Beef Shabu Shabu with Ponzu
      Dipping Sauce 255–6
  sourcing 266–7
Keaton, Diane 42

INDEX

Keitel, Harvey 193
Kelly, Gene 75
Kessel, Sam 169
Keynes, Skandar 30
Kidman, Nicole 203
kirschwasser
    California Dreamin' Cocktail 208
    sourcing 267
    Wire-cutter Cocktail 229
Kleiser, Randal 78
kombu
    Beef Shabu Shabu with Ponzu
        Dipping Sauce 255–6
    sourcing 267
Kubrick, Stanley 243
Kuroki, Hitomi 253

Laye, Dilys 107
Ledger, Heath 223
Lee, Ang xiii, 223
Lee, Christopher 21, 239
Leigh, Vivien 130
Lembas Bread 29
Lemmon, Jack 137
Lenya, Lotte 54
lesbian films see gay and lesbian
    films
Lester, Mark 69
light bites see snacks
Lillet Blanc 52–3, 267–8
Lingren, Lisa 169
Lion, the Witch and the Wardrobe,
    The (2005) 30–1
Liotta, Ray 7
Liquorice Toffee Apples 212–13
Lithgow, John 214
Liver with Fava Beans and Chianti
    85–6
Lloyd, David 72
Loaves and Fishes 101–2

Lobsters, Steamed, with Beurre
    Blanc 43–4
Lord of the Rings, The trilogy xiv,
    21–9
loundza 269
Lucas, George 117
Lumpfish Caviare
    Devilled Eggs with 114–16
    sourcing 268
Lynch, David 51, 200

MacLachlan, Kyle 148, 200
Madonna 145
Madsen, Michael 193
Maguire, Sharon 45
mains
    Adobo Marinated Trout with
        Corn Salsa 198–9
    Ancient Roman Barley Stew
        181–2
    Asio-Caribbean Papaya Steak
        59–60
    Beef Shabu Shabu with Ponzu
        Dipping Sauce 255–6
    Buttermilk Fried Chicken 131–2
    Char-grilled Baby Octopus 147
    Chicory and Ham Gratin 163–4
    Clemenza's Sicilian Meatballs 5–6
    Doe Schnitzels 73–4
    Elk and Bean Stew 225–6
    Gourmet Doggie Chow 150
    Liver with Fava Beans and Chianti
        85–6
    Loaves and Fishes 101–2
    Pork Loin with Prunes and
        Caraway 171–2
    Rabbit and Root Stew 26
    Rebel Meatloaf 134–6
    Roast Long Pig with Coca-Cola
        Gravy 237–8

mains (*cont.*)
  Salt-grilled Sea Bream with
      Wakame Salad 251–2
  Sardinian Mullet Escabeche
      63
  Sole in White Wine 55–6
  Steak Tartare 195
  Steamed Lobsters with Beurre
      Blanc 43–4
Mango Daiquiris 232
Manilow, Barry 10
Marceau, Sophie 188
marrow bones, Gourmet Doggie
    Chow 150
Martini
  Arctic Martini Granita 66
  Vesper Lynd 53
Mastrantonio, Mary Elizabeth 15
Maura, Carmen 173
McCormack, Catherine 188
McDowell, Malcolm 243
McGoohan, Patrick 187
McKean, Michael 103
McKellen, Ian 21
Meatballs, Clemenza's Sicilian 5–6
Meatloaf, Rebel 134–6
Meloni, Christopher 228
meringues, Frozen Raspberry Tits
    138–9
Miike, Takashi 249
Mikkelsen, Mads 51
milky recipes
  Coconut Frogspawn 216
  Moloko Drencom 245
Miller, Jason 94
Mineo, Sal 133
Minogue, Kylie 231
Mint Chocolate Mousse, Chalky 89
Misery (1990) xiii
Miyazaki, Hayao 217

Moloko Drencom 245
Monroe, Marilyn 137
Monty Python's Life of Brian (1979)
    99–100
Moodysson, Lukas 169
Moore, Julianne 197, 206
Moore, Roger 61
Mortensen, Viggo 27
Mousse, Chalky Mint Chocolate 89
muffin cases 268
Muffins, Cinnamon Crusted
      Blueberry 12–13
Murphy, Eddie 215
mushrooms
  Beef Shabu Shabu with Ponzu
      Dipping Sauce 255–6
  Doe Schnitzels 73–4
  enokitake 255–6, 266
  Prawn and Mushroom Wonton
      167–8
  Tatooine Mushrooms Skewers
      119–20
musicals 67–80
Myers, Mike 214

Nakata, Hideo 253
Newell, Mike 33
Newton-John, Olivia 78
Noble, John 27
Nyqvist, Mikael 170

oats, Atholl Brose 189–90
O'Brien, Richard 236
octopus
  Char-grilled Baby Octopus 147
  sourcing 268
Oliver! (1968) 69–70
Olivier, Laurence 75
orange, Chocolate Orange Angel-
    food Cake 76–7

INDEX

orange liqueur
  Mango Daiquiris 232
  Wire-cutter Cocktail 229
Osbourne, Ozzy 27
Osso Buco with Razored Garlic
  Gremolata 8–9
Otto, Miranda 28

Pacino, Al 3, 14
Palin, Michael 100
Pantoliano, Joe 227
Pasties, Pumpkin 34–5
Pearce, Guy 230
Penn, Chris 197
Peppard, George 141
Pesci, Joe 8, 11
Pfeiffer, Michelle 14, 15
Phoenix, Joaquin 179
Pie, Cranberry and Apple 204–5
pineapple juice
  Bubble Royale Fruity Pearl Tea
    259–60
  California Dreamin' Cocktail 208
pistachio nuts
  Pistachio and Coconut Turkish
    Delight 31–2
  Soylent Green Halva Macaroon
    Squares 123–4
Pitof 151
Plummer, Christopher 72
Poésy, Clémence 33
Polanski, Roman 87
Popcorn, Bloody 92
pork
  Clemenza's Sicilian Meatballs
    5–6
  loin 159–60, 171–2, 269
  Pork Loin with Prunes and
    Caraway 171–2

Roast Long Pig with Coca-Cola
  Gravy 237–8
Solyanka Soup 159–60
Spartan Black Soup 185–6
porridge, Atholl Brose 189–90
Prawn and Mushroom Wonton
  167–8
Prowse, David 117
prunes
  Fruit Gruel 70–1
  Pork Loin with Prunes and
    Caraway 171–2
Psycho (1960) xiii
Pumpkin Pasties 34–5

Quinn, Patricia 236

Rabbit and Root Stew 26
Radcliffe, Daniel 33
Raspberry Tits, Frozen 138–9
Ray, Nicholas 133
razzies 143–53
Rebel Meatloaf 134–6
Rebel without a Cause (1955)
  133–4
red snapper, Loaves and Fishes
  101–2
Reed, Carol 69
Reed, Oliver 180
Reilly, John C. 206
Reiner, Rob 39, 103
Rennies 89
Reservoir Dogs (1992) 193–4
Reynolds, Burt 206
Reynolds, Debbie 75
Rice and Bean Cakes, Japanese
  (Daifuku) 219–20
Ritchie, Guy 145
Roast Gammon Sandwiches with
  Cumberland Sauce 105–6

INDEX

Roast Long Pig with Coca-Cola
    Gravy 237–8
Robbins, Tim 197
Rocky Horror Picture Show, The
    (1975) 235–7
romantic comedy 37–48
Rooney, Mickey 140
Root and Rabbit Stew 26
Rosemary's Baby (1968) 87–8
rosewater 32, 268–9
Rossellini, Isabella 200
Roth, Tim 193–4
rum
    Fruit Gruel 70–1
    white, Mango Daiquiris 232
Ryan, Meg xiv, 39

Salad, Wakame, Salt-grilled Sea
    Bream with 251–2
Salsa, Corn, Adobo Marinated Trout
    with 198–9
Salt-grilled Sea Bream with Wakame
    Salad 251–2
Samuelsson, Emma 169
Sandwiches, Roast Gammon, with
    Cumberland Sauce 105–6
Santoro, Rodrigo 183
Sarandon, Susan 235
Sardinian Mullet Escabeche 63
Sass, Katrin 157
sauces
    Adobo sauce 198–9
    Cumberland Sauce 105–6
    dipping 119–20
    fruit 109–10
    Madeira 150
    for meatballs 5–6
    ponzu dipping sauce 255–6
    for Prawn and Mushroom
        Wonton 167–8

rémoulade 114–16
Saucy Crumpet 109–10
sausages, kabanos 159–60,
    266
Scarface (1983) 14–15
science fiction 111–24
Scorsese, Martin 7, 10
Scorupco, Izabella 64
Scott, Ridley 113, 179, 180
Scott, Terry 107
Scream (1996) 90–2
sea bass, Casablancan Fish Soup
    129
Sea Bream, Salt-grilled, with
    Wakame Salad 251–2
seaweed *see* wakame
Secombe, Harry 69
semolina flour, Lembas Bread 29
Serrano, Julieta 174
Sharman, Jim 235
Shiina, Eihi 249
Short Cuts (1993) 196–8
Showgirls (1995) xii, 148–9
Shrek (2001) 214–15
Silence of the Lambs (1991) xii,
    83–4
Sims, Joan 107
Singin' in the Rain (1952) 75–6
Smith, Brooke 84
snacks
    Caraway and Horseradish
        Coleslaw 41
    Japanese Rice and Bean Cakes
        (Daifuku) 219–20
    Roast Gammon Sandwiches with
        Cumberland Sauce 105–6
Snow White and the Seven Dwarf's
    (1937) 211–12
Snyder, Zack 183
Sole in White Wine 55–6

INDEX

Solyanka Soup 159–60
Solyent Green (1973) 121–2
Solyent Green Halva Macaroon
    Squares 123–4
Some Like it Hot (1959) 137–8
Sorvino, Paul 8
Sound of Music, The (1965)
    72–3
soups
    Blue Soup 47–8
    Casablancan Fish Soup 129
    Gazpacho 175–6
    Solyanka Soup 159–60
    Spartan Black Soup 185–6
Spartan Black Soup 185–6
Spiced Shire Ale 23
Spirited Away (2001) 217–18
Spy Who Loved Me, The (1977)
    61–2
Stamp, Terence 230
Star Wars Episode IV: A New Hope
    (1977) 117–19
starters
    Casablancan Fish Soup 129
    Devilled Eggs with Lumpfish
        Caviare 114–16
    Prawn and Mushroom Wonton
        167–8
    Tatooine Mushrooms Skewers
        119–20
steak
    Asio-Caribbean Papaya Steak
        59–60
    Beef Shabu Shabu with Ponzu
        Dipping Sauce 255–6
    Gourmet Doggie Chow 150
    Steak Tartare 195
Steamed Lobsters with Beurre Blanc
    43–4
stews

Ancient Roman Barley Stew
    181–2
    Elk and Bean Stew 225–6
    Rabbit and Root Stew 26
Stone, Sharon 10, 152
Stowe, Madeleine 197
sugar thermometers 16, 32, 213
sultanas 70–1
sweets
    Liquorice Toffee Apples
        212–13
    Pistachio and Coconut Turkish
        Delight 31–2
Swept Away (2002) 145–6
Swinton, Tilda 30

Takeshi, Beat 257
tapioca
    Bubble Royale Fruity Pearl Tea
        259–60
    Coconut Frogspawn 216
    sourcing 269
Tarantino, Quentin 193
Tatooine Mushrooms Skewers
    119–20
Tautou, Audrey 161
Taxi Driver (1976) xiii
Taylor-Young, Leigh 122
Tea, Bubble Royale Fruity Pearl
    259–60
This is Spinal Tap (1984) 103–4
Thomas, Gerald 107
Tierney, Lawrence 193
Tilly, Jennifer 227
To Die For (1995) 203–4
Tocino de Cielo (Cuban Gold Bar)
    16–17
Toffee Apples, Liquorice 212–13
tofu, Prawn and Mushroom Wonton
    167–8

INDEX

Together (2000) 169–70
tomatoes
  Adobo Marinated Trout with
    Corn Salsa 198–9
  Gazpacho 175–6
Tomlin, Lily 196
Travolta, John 78
Trout, Adobo Marinated, with Corn
  Salsa 198–9
Trump, Donald 183
Turkish Delight, Pistachio and
  Coconut 31–2
Two Towers, The (2002) 24–5

Van Sant, Gus 203
veal
  Clemenza's Sicilian Meatballs
    5–6
  Osso Buco with Razored Garlic
    Gremolta 8–9
vegetable soup, Blue 47–8
venison, Doe Schnitzels 73–4
vermouth, Arctic Martini Granita
  66
Vesper Lynd Martini 53
vodka
  Arctic Martini Granita 66
  California Dreamin' Cocktail
    208
  Vesper Lynd Martini 53
von Sydow, Max 94

Wahlberg, Mark 206
Wakame

Salad, Salt-grilled Sea Bream with
  251–2
  sourcing 269–70
Ward, Fred 196
Watson, Emma 33
Weaver, Sigourney 114
Weaving, Hugo 230
When Harry Met Sally (1989) xiv,
  39–40
Whisky and Ginger Wicker Man
  241–2
White Wine, Sole in 55–6
Wicker Man, The (1973) 239–40
Wilder, Billy 137
William, Prince 69
Williams, Kenneth 108
Wilson, Dooley 127
Windsor, Barbara 108
Wire-cutter Cocktail 229
Wise, Robert 72
Wiseman, Joseph 57
*Women on the Verge of a Nervous
  Breakdown* (1988) 173–4
wonton wrappers, sourcing 270
Wontons, Prawn and Mushroom
  167–8
Wood, Elijah 21
Wood, Natalie 133
Woodward, Edward 239
wormwood 263

Young, Terence 54, 57

Zellweger, Renée 45